The
Private Prayers of
POPE
JOHN PAUL II

The Rosary Hour

Joannes Paulus II

The Private Prayers of Pope John Paul II

Words of Inspiration

An Invitation to Prayer

The Rosary Hour

*The
Private Prayers of*
POPE
JOHN PAUL II

The Rosary Hour

ATRIA BOOKS
New York London Toronto Sydney Singapore

ATRIA BOOKS
1230 Avenue of the Americas
New York, NY 10020

ISBN: 0-7434-4440-X

First Atria Books hardcover printing October 2002

10 9 8 7 6 5 4 3 2 1

ATRIA BOOKS is a trademark of Simon & Schuster, Inc.

For information regarding special discounts for bulk purchases,
please contact Simon & Schuster Special Sales at 1-800-456-6798 or
business@simonandschuster.com

Printed in the U.S.A.

EDITOR'S NOTE

This edition is a translation of the original work, *L'ora del Rosario (The Rosary Hour)*, published in Italian in the Vatican City State. Like the previous books in this series, *Words of Inspiration* and *An Invitation to Prayer*, *The Rosary Hour* retains the organization of the original.

CONTENTS

INTRODUCTION

A few days after his election to the papacy, John Paul II confided to the faithful in St. Peter's Square:

> "The Rosary is my favorite prayer.
> It is a marvelous prayer!
> Marvelous in its simplicity
> and in its profundity."

OCTOBER 29, 1978

and again:

> "It is a daily encounter
> that Our Lady and I never miss:
> If you want to be near the Pope's heart
> for a few moments,
> I suggest the Rosary hour,
> when I remember all of you to the Virgin Mary,
> and I would be pleased if you would remember
>   me to her
> in the same way."

MAY 12, 1991

Many times in the course of his papacy, John Paul II has urged the faithful to recite the Rosary.

This volume is a collection of the Pope's comments on the Rosary, made during his addresses during the Wednesday general audience, and during his pastoral journeys in Italy and abroad.

It also offers, as an aid, some Rosary meditations presented by the Holy Father on particular occasions.

May the Pope's love for and attachment to the Rosary arouse in our Christian communities renewed faithfulness to this form of prayer, which is cherished by Christian piety and is always relevant.

A SIMPLE PRAYER

The Rosary is a simple prayer, reflecting the soul of Mary, who, in her spiritual richness, is of a perfect simplicity. In this sense, the Rosary helps us to simplify our prayers and all our contact with the heavenly world; it enables us to advance in a simplicity that sincerely expresses the depths of our soul.

The Rosary can be called a prayer of the poor, because it is a prayer without pretenses; it is a prayer in which the Christian, though he is aware of his spiritual misery, is never lost: the more unworthy he feels of being in the presence of the purity and greatness of the Virgin Mary, the more ardently he can pray for her intercession and her protection.

Although the Rosary is a prayer of the poor, it is not a poor prayer, because it is rich in all the mystery of salvation that it expresses. Invoking Mary "full of grace," the Christian sits before the Virgin of Nazareth, who has received that eulogy in the angel's message. He recognizes in her the fullness of grace that inaugurated the coming of the Savior into the world. His coming was accomplished in that single moment when Mary gave her consent to the divine proposal.

It is precisely the gift of fullness of grace that allowed Mary to welcome the divine will into her existence unconditionally. Having received grace from the first moment of her life, she was always open to God's wishes. At the moment of the Annunciation, Mary assumed the attitude that was habitual to her: full acceptance of the divine plan, without the least reserve. Thus the profound simplicity of her soul was confirmed. That simplicity lay in her perfect accord with God's intentions.

To better understand the value of this simplicity, it is enough to reflect on the complications that enter our life when we separate ourselves from the divine will. From the moment we try to find something other than this will, endeavoring to fulfill our desires or seeking, everywhere, our satisfactions, we come up against all kinds of obstacles, and our life turns complicated: We are necessarily torn between the sovereign exigencies of God and the aspirations that would remove us from them. We forfeit our inner peace and set off on dead-end paths.

When we look at Mary, calling her "full of grace," we find ourselves in the presence of a soul that maintained its simplicity. In her inmost attitudes, there was no deviation: everything was of a luminous clarity, and all was transparent to the divine will that was brought to fulfillment in her life.

No conflict could occur in her, no protests, reproaches, or opposition to God's designs.

Of course, this doesn't mean that Mary didn't have any problems. At the Annunciation, she wondered how she could become a mother, as it had been announced to her, since she wished to remain a virgin, and she did not hesitate to ask the angel. But after the response telling her how she would bear the child who was to be the Messiah, Mary declared her total willingness. She realized that the ideal solution to our problems comes from on high, and we must know how to accept it.

Turning our gaze toward Mary as we say the Rosary, we have a chance to enter more profoundly into the simplicity of this soul full of grace. In admiring Mary, who consistently aligned her desires and her will with the divine will, we learn to follow her example. To contemplate Mary in her simplicity means wishing to share that simplicity, because it is accessible to us, too, if we adopt the same conformity to the divine will.

The Rosary reminds us ceaselessly of the exceptional greatness of the Virgin, the Mother of God, but it also helps us to understand that even if we do not receive a grace so extraordinary we are beneficiaries of a grace that leads us to live in harmony with God. This grace allows us to simplify our life more and more, in peace and in joy.

JEAN GALOT*

---

*Catholic theologian

What Is the Rosary?

The Rosary, a prayer so simple and yet so rich

I wish to draw your attention to the Rosary. In the Church, in fact, October is the month dedicated to the Rosary.

> The Rosary is my favorite prayer.
> It is a marvelous prayer!
> Marvelous in its simplicity
> and in its profundity.

In this prayer we repeat over and over again the words that were spoken to the Virgin Mary by the angel and by her kinswoman Elizabeth. The entire Church shares in these words. One might say that the Rosary is, in a certain sense, a comment-prayer on the last chapter of the Constitution *Lumen Gentium* of the Second Vatican Council, a chapter that treats of the miraculous presence of the Mother of God in the mystery of Christ and the Church. In fact, against the background of the words "Hail Mary," the principal episodes of the life of Jesus Christ pass before the eyes of the soul. Together they compose Joyful, Sorrowful, and Glorious Mysteries, and put us in living communion with Jesus through—we might say—the Heart of his Mother. At the same time our heart contains in these decades of the Rosary all the events that make up the life of the individual, of the family, of the nation, of the Church, and of humanity. Our personal actions and the actions of our neighbors and, especially, of those who are closest to us, who are most in our hearts. In this way the simple prayer of the Rosary beats out the rhythm of human life.

In recent weeks I have had the chance to meet many people, representing many diverse nations and milieus, many churches and Christian communities. I wish to assure you that I did not fail to translate these relationships into the language of the Rosary, so that all might find themselves in the heart of the prayer that gives a full dimension to everything.

In recent weeks I have received, through the Holy See, numerous proofs of goodwill on the part of people from all over the world. I want to express my gratitude in decades of the Rosary, so that I can show it not only personally but in prayer — in *this prayer that is so simple and yet so rich. I warmly urge you all to recite it.*

OCTOBER 29, 1978

Mankind needs Mary!

Mankind needs Mary! In her we find, truly, access to the heart of her Son, the only place where our restlessness can find peace, where our sorrows find comfort, where our intentions to live a life consistent with the values of the Gospel find strength and constancy.

Pray fervently to Most Holy Mary! Be aware of her at your side and consecrate yourselves to her, renewing throughout the day your affection and your trust, so that she may accompany you in your daily affairs. Her memory is alive in families, especially in the daily recitation of the Rosary. It's a daily encounter that she and I never miss: if you wish to be close to the heart of the Pope for some moments, I suggest to you the Rosary hour, when I remember all of you to the Virgin Mary, and I would be pleased if you would remember me to her in the same way.

MAY 12, 1991

My adoration of the Most High, with Mary, and with the beloved pilgrims of Fatima, is joined in an act of grace, which I hope may continue to be, for all of you, communion and life: Rosary in hand, the sweet name of the Mother on our lips, and the song of Love—the Lord's mercy—in our heart. *"My spirit rejoices in God my Savior."* For me the date of May 13 will forever evoke the special maternal protection of Our Lady, and a debt of gratitude that recent events have only increased; but I continue to say, with Mary and for Most Holy Mary, *"Thanks to the Lord... whose mercy is never exhausted."*

MAY 13, 1983

In the Rosary we bless the faith of Mary

"And blessed is she who believed."

Blessed are you, O Mary, who believed, when the Messenger of God spoke to you.

Blessed are you, who believed *"that there would be a fulfillment of what was spoken to her from the Lord."*

Elizabeth blesses your faith.

The entire Church blesses your faith.

All humanity blesses your faith.

All of us who recite the Holy Rosary *bless the faith of Mary,* in each of its Mysteries.

Let us pray to her.

And let us pray together with her.

We believe that in these Mysteries she prays with us. Mary allows us to find ourselves *amid the great things* that the Almighty has accomplished in her, amid the *"great works of God"* through which the Church lives.

Like a mother she guides the life in which the Church's faith, hope, and charity are expressed.

And this happens — in a special way — *through the Holy Rosary.*

Let us give thanks for all the fruits of this prayer, through which the Mother of Christ has been with us.

OCTOBER 28, 1984

The Rosary, the summary of the whole Gospel

As you know, tomorrow is the start of the month of October, which Christian piety has linked, in particular, to a more committed and devout daily recitation of the Holy Rosary, which my predecessors Pius XII and Paul VI called *the summary of the whole Gospel.*" For centuries this prayer has held an honored place in the worship of the Blessed Virgin, *"under whose protection the faithful, praying, take refuge in all dangers and times of need."*

The Rosary is a simple prayer but at the same time theologically rich in Biblical references; for this reason Christians love it and recite it frequently and fervently, well aware of its authentic "Gospel nature," which Paul VI speaks of in the Apostolic Exhortation on the worship of the Blessed Virgin.

In the Rosary we meditate on the principal events of salvation that were accomplished in Christ: from the virgin conception to the final moments of the Passion and the glorification of the Mother of God. This is a prayer of continuous praise and supplication to Most Holy Mary, that she may intercede for us, poor sinners, in every moment of our day, until the hour of our death.

So I wish to urge you, in the month of October, to rediscover the Holy Rosary and to value it more highly as a personal and family prayer, addressed to she who is the Mother of faithful individuals and the Mother of the Church.

SEPTEMBER 30, 1981

The Rosary is the memory of the Redemption

Among the many aspects of the Rosary that Popes, Saints, and scholars have revealed, one in particular should be noted. The Holy Rosary is a continuous memory of the Redemption, in its crucial stages: the Incarnation of the Word, his Passion and Death for us, Easter, which he initiated for us and which will be fulfilled eternally in Heaven.

If, then, we consider the contemplative elements of the Rosary, that is, the Mysteries around which the spoken prayer unwinds, we can better understand why this crown of *Hail Marys* has been called "The Psalter of the Virgin." As the Psalms reminded Israel of the marvels of the Exodus and of the salvation wrought by God, and served as a constant admonition to be faithful to the pact made on Sinai, so the Rosary continuously recalls to us the new Covenant of the prodigies of mercy and the power that God has revealed in Christ on behalf of men, and reminds us to be faithful to our baptismal pledges. We are his people, he is our God.

But this reminder of God's miracles and this constant call to faith passes, in a sense, through Mary, the faithful Virgin. The succession of *Hail Marys* helps us to penetrate, from one time to the next, ever deeper into the most profound mystery of the Word Incarnate and Savior, *"with the heart of her who was closest to the Lord."* Because Mary, too, as a Daughter of Zion and heir to the wise spirituality of Israel, sang the miracles of the Exodus; but, as the first and most perfect disciple of Christ, she walked through and experienced the Passover of the New Covenant, storing it in her heart and meditating on every word and gesture of her Son, joining him with unconditional faith, and indicating to all the path of the new pact: "Do whatever he tells you." Glorified today in Heaven, she demonstrates in herself the journey of the new people to the promised land.

The Rosary thus immerses us in the mysteries of Christ, and offers his Mother to every one of the faithful and to all the Church as the perfect model of how to accept, cherish, and live every word and deed of God, on the ongoing journey to the salvation of the world.

OCTOBER 9, 1983

The Rosary: prayer of solidarity

In this month of October, traditionally consecrated to the Holy Rosary, I wish to dedicate the Angelus address to this prayer, which is so dear to Catholic hearts, so much loved by me, and so warmly recommended by my predecessor Popes.

In this extraordinary Holy Year of the Redemption, even the Rosary acquires new perspectives and is charged with stronger and broader aims than in the past. Today it's not a matter of asking for great victories in war, as at Lepanto or Vienna; rather, it's a matter of asking Mary to make us brave fighters against the spirit of error and evil, with the weapons of the Gospel, which are the Cross and the Word of God.

The prayer of the Rosary is the prayer of man for man: it is the prayer of human solidarity, the joint prayer of the redeemed, which reflects the spirit and purpose of Mary, the Mother and image of the Church, who was the first to be redeemed. It is a prayer for all the people of the world and of history, alive or dead, called to be with us the Body of Christ and to become with him the heirs of the Father's glory.

If we consider the spiritual orientations suggested by the Rosary, which is a simple, Gospel prayer, we find again the intentions that St. Cipriano noted in the Our Father. He wrote: "The Lord, Master of peace and unity, did not want us to pray individually and alone. We do not in fact say: 'My Father, who art in Heaven'; or 'Give me this day my daily bread.' Our prayer is for all, so that, when we pray, we do it not for one alone but for all people, because we are one with all people."

The Rosary is addressed consistently to she who is the highest expression of humanity in prayer, the model of the Church asking and praying, in Christ, for the mercy of the Father. As Christ is "always ready to intercede in our behalf," Mary, too, continues in Heaven her mission as the Mother and becomes the voice of every man for every man, until the final crowning of the band of the elect. Praying to her, we ask her to assist us through the whole arc of our present life and, above all, in that moment of decision for our eternal destiny, which will be "the hour of our death."

The Rosary is a prayer that points to the prospect of the Kingdom of God and orients man to receive the fruits of Redemption.

OCTOBER 2, 1983

The Rosary brings God into our lives

The prayer of the Rosary is a great help to men and women in our time. It brings peace and meditation; it introduces our lives to the Mysteries of God and brings God into our lives. Our thoughts and feelings are little by little freed from anxiety and from the transience of our problems and interests and become more and more open to the action of God.

The words we recite can occupy our whole attention; but they willingly draw back and become an external frame that routs fatigue and distraction, a background melody that resonates in us.

It would be a great joy for me if participation in the recitation of the Rosary together with the successor of St. Peter became an occasion for you to become seriously involved in this form of meditative prayer. It also represents a good opportunity to experience communion. In times of need it gives strength and clarity to our prayer.

SEPTEMBER 3, 1983

Pius XII defined the Rosary as "a summary of the whole Gospel." In its wise yet simple structure, it offers themes for meditation from the story of the journey of Christ and Mary, through the Mysteries of Joy, Sorrow, and Glory. The prayers of the Our Father and the Hail Mary also bear the imprint of the Gospel. The insistence, then, on the repetition of these prayers is a recognition of our human neediness, and, at the same time, the expression of our unshakable faith in the help that comes to us from on high and particularly from the maternal intercession of the Virgin.

The Rosary, which provides fruitful nourishment for personal piety, is in a certain sense the typical prayer of the Christian family. The Second Vatican Council called the Christian family the "domestic church," with the intention of highlighting the authentically ecclesial sacred reality that is established in the family environment. Moreover, the family is called upon to make itself into the image of the Church of Christ. In the recitation of the Rosary it experiences its own unity, enjoys the flow of affections, and rises to contemplation of the divine, placing in this superior dimension its own needs, and the difficulties and the achievements of daily life.

The Queen of the Holy Rosary is honored especially in the remarkable sanctuary of Pompeii, where today, at this noon hour, the ancient "Petition" is recited, in which the populations of Italy are spiritually joined. To this chorus of entreaty we add, dearest young people, our fervent invocation:

O blessed Rosary of Mary,
sweet chain that unites us to God,
chain of love that unites us to the angels.

Tower of salvation against the assaults of Hell.
Safe harbor in the universal shipwreck,
we will never abandon you.
You will be our comfort in the hour of death,
to you the last kiss
of our dying life.
And the final word on our lips
will be your sweet name,
O Queen of the Rosary of Pompeii,
O dearest Mother,
O refuge of sinners,
O sovereign comforter of the afflicted.
Be everywhere blessed, today and forever,
on earth and in Heaven.
Amen.

OCTOBER 7, 1984

The simplicity and the profundity of the Rosary

Now, at the end of October, I would like, along with you, my brothers and sisters, to examine the simultaneous simplicity and profundity of this prayer, to which the Most Holy Mother invites us, urges us, and encourages us. In reciting the Rosary, we penetrate the Mysteries of the life of Jesus, which are at the same time the Mysteries of his Mother.

This can be seen clearly in the Joyful Mysteries, beginning with the Annunciation, through the Visitation and the birth on that night in Bethlehem, and later in the presentation of the Lord, until he is found in the temple, when he was already twelve years old.

Although it may seem that the Sorrowful Mysteries do not directly show us the Mother of Jesus — with the exception of the last two: the Via Crucis and the Crucifixion — how could we even imagine that the Mother was spiritually absent when her Son was suffering so terribly in Gethsemane, during his scourging and crowning with thorns?

And the Glorious Mysteries are in fact Mysteries of Christ, in which we find the *spiritual presence* of Mary — and first of all is the Mystery of the Resurrection. The Holy Scripture does not mention the presence of Mary when it describes the Ascension — but must she not be present, if immediately afterward we read that she was in the Upper Room with the Apostles themselves, who had just said farewell to Christ as he rose to Heaven? Together with them, Mary prepared for the coming of the Holy Spirit and shared in the Pentecost of his descent. The last two Glorious Mysteries direct our thoughts toward the Mother of God, when we contemplate her Assumption and coronation in celestial glory.

The Rosary is a prayer *about Mary* united with Christ in his mission as the Savior. At the same time it is a prayer *to Mary*—our best mediator with her Son. It is, finally, a prayer that in a special way we say *with Mary,* just as the Apostles at the Last Supper prayed with her, preparing to receive the Holy Spirit.

OCTOBER 28, 1981

Let us take up again the crown of the Rosary

Our thoughts turn today to the sanctuary of the Blessed Virgin of the Rosary in Pompeii, a sanctuary very dear to Dr. Moscati, whom I had the joy of proclaiming a saint this morning. He stayed there frequently on his journeys to Amalfi, Salerno, and Campobasso to visit the sick or in other circumstances. *"How sweet it is,"* he confided to an acquaintance, *"to take communion in the Sanctuary of Pompeii! At the feet of Our Lady it seems to me that I become more humble and tell her things as they are."*

We, too, wish today to take ourselves spiritually to that Center of Marian devotion, to open our hearts to Our Lady and tell her *"things as they are."* The Sanctuary of Pompeii, with its vast, international resonance, with the multitudes of pilgrims who flow to it, with the great complex of works that surround it, bears witness to the powerful energies that the worship of Mary rouses, energies that are definitely translated into passionate love for mankind, all mankind, in the spiritual dimension as well as in the social and temporal dimensions.

Fundamental to the works of Bartolo Longo is, as we know, love for mankind for, the men and women who suffered in the Valle di Pompeii at the end of the nineteenth century, brutalized by a life of hardship and ignorance.

Bartolo Longo understood that what that impoverished people needed most was the Catechism, along with the maternal and merciful presence of Mary, which became more accessible through a humble portrait of Our Lady of the Rosary, placed in the little church in the Valle di Pompeii on November 13, 1875.

This very portrait will soon become the fulcrum, as it were, of a religious and charitable movement on an international scale. According to the enlightened ideas of Bartolo Longo, Marian devotion and the pious recitation of the Rosary would be an extraordinarily effective means of advancement and universal peace not only for the poor peasants of the Valle di Pompeii but for the whole Church and all of society. We wish today to welcome the call that comes to us from Blessed Bartolo Longo, and from the new Saint, Dr. Giuseppe Moscati, for a renewed commitment to devotion to Mary. Our Lady of Pompeii, venerated under the title of Virgin of the Rosary, shows us a privileged means of progressing in devotion to her and deepening our relationship of faith and love toward her Son Jesus: the Crown of the Rosary.

The contemplation of the Mysteries in which the story of our salvation is bound up, the invocation to God the Father with the very words that Jesus taught us, the rhythmic flow of the Hail Mary, like a garland of roses twining around the purest, most beautiful, most holy of all women, the final glorification of the divine Trinity—all these make the Rosary a prayer that is extraordinarily rich in content, yet contained within a simple structure that allows it to be recited in varied circumstances.

Let us again take up in our hands, dearest brothers and sisters, the Crown of the Rosary, to express our veneration for Mary, to learn from her to be diligent disciples of the divine Teacher, to pray for his celestial assistance as much in our daily needs as in the great problems that anguish the Church and all humanity.

OCTOBER 25, 1987

The Rosary. This prayer, which has its origins in the Diocese of Essen, is still for many men and women today a sign of and a means to a more intimate communion with Christ. Those who have endured hard times, distress, solitude, and sickness, those who are facing death, have always found in the Rosary consolation, comfort, and new strength. We, today, in full consciousness, wish to join the ranks of those who have dedicated themselves to the Rosary through the centuries. Mary, the Mother of Jesus and our Mother, helps us not to lose sight of Christ, if like her we open ourselves to the Word of God, and, answering the call, let ourselves be conquered by Christ. In this, I, too, accompany you with my special prayer and blessing.

MAY 2, 1987

Spreading the recitation of the Rosary

The month of October is dedicated to the Rosary. I would urge you to recite this prayer, reminding you of a passage on the Rosary that my venerable predecessor, Paul VI, wrote, in the Apostolic Exhortation *Marialis Cultus.*

"As a Gospel prayer centered on the Mystery of the Redemptive Incarnation, the Rosary is a prayer clearly oriented to Christ. In fact, its characteristic element—the litanylike succession of Hail Marys—also becomes unceasing praise of Christ, who is the ultimate object of the angel's announcement and of the greeting of the mother of John the Baptist: 'Blessed is the fruit of your womb.' We will say more: the repetition of the Hail Mary constitutes the warp on which the contemplation of the Mysteries is woven: the Jesus whom each Hail Mary recalls is the same Jesus whom the succession of the Mysteries presents to us—now as the son of God, now as the son of the Virgin—at his birth in a stable in Bethlehem; at his presentation by his Mother in the temple; as a youth full of zeal for his Father's affairs; as the Redeemer in agony in the garden; scourged and crowned with thorns; carrying the Cross and dying on Calvary; risen from the dead and ascended to the glory of the Father, to send forth the gift of the Spirit."

The month of October unites us with the Queen of the Holy Rosary in this blessed prayer. In this month may the Rosary spread. Mary wishes to pray with us for the salvation of mankind and of the threatened world.

SEPTEMBER 30, 1984

The feast of the Holy Rosary

The Church urges us to renew in our souls love for the Marian *crown*.

I wish to dwell on this pious practice, so deeply rooted in the heart of Christian people and so strongly urged by my predecessors, who encouraged its dissemination, expounding on the theological and spiritual aspects of it, as a prayer of both praise and supplication. Pope Leo XIII wrote in his Encyclical *Octobri Mense*: "The contemplation of these august Mysteries, contemplated in their order, affords to faithful souls a wonderful confirmation of faith, protection against the disease of error, and increase of the strength of the soul."

To recite the Rosary in fact means enrolling in the school of Mary and learning from her, the Mother and Disciple of Christ, how to live deeply and fully the requirements of Christian faith — she was the first believer, the first to have an ecclesial life, she who in the Upper Room was the center of unity and love among the first Disciples of her Son.

Reciting the Holy Rosary is not a matter of repeating formulas but, rather, of entering into confidential *conversation* with Mary, *speaking to her,* showing her our hopes, confiding our pain, opening our heart to her, declaring to her our willingness to accept the plan of God, promising faithfulness to her in all circumstances, and especially those which are difficult and painful, sure of her protection and certain that she will obtain for us from her Son the grace necessary for our salvation.

In fact, in reciting the Holy Rosary we contemplate Christ from a privileged perspective, that is, from the perspective of

Mary, his Mother; we meditate on the Mysteries of the life, the Passion, and the Resurrection of the Lord with the eyes and the heart of she who was closest to her Son.

We are assiduous in reciting the Rosary both in the ecclesial community and in the intimacy of our families: with repeated invocations, it will unite hearts, rekindle the domestic hearth, fortify our hope, and obtain for all the peace and joy of Christ who was born, died, and rose for us.

OCTOBER 2, 1988

We need to pray and to praise Mary

The Rosary remains a simple and effective prayer so that with Mary we may become disciples of Jesus Christ. To know Jesus Christ, to meditate and renew in our lives each of his Mysteries, is the theme of Father Chevrier. In this prayer that the Church ceaselessly urges, as does the Virgin herself in her apparitions, like those of Lourdes, the Mysteries of Jesus are followed with the eyes and heart of Mary. Further, Father Chevrier, as a good apostle to the poor, suggests to them this prayer in particular.

And how can we ever forget that it was Paolina Jaricot in Lyon who had the idea of the fifteen-member groups of the *Living Rosary,* just as she launched the Work for the Propagation of the Faith? In a few years, she was able to unite millions of people in France and in many other countries in a broad chain of solidarity, to meditate in turn on the Joyful, Sorrowful, and Glorious Mysteries, and to pray in accordance with the grand intentions of the Church: the salvation of sinners, and missions. She succeeded, as she herself put it, in *"making the Rosary a pleasure for the masses."*

Today there is the same need to praise Mary, to pray to her, to be available, like her, to the Holy Spirit, and to perform the work of her Son. It is a matter of educating the faithful, families, and children.

OCTOBER 4, 1986

Pray faithfully to the Most Holy Virgin, who wants only our earthly and eternal good; recite the Rosary in your families and in your parishes, praying insistently for perseverance in faith, in grace, in charity and the conversion of the dispossessed. Certainly Redemption includes the sufferings on the Cross and the adversities of the world; yet Mary is always present in the tribulations of human history and in the travails of our individual existence.

Let us recall the incisive words of the Second Vatican Council, which should be for all of us a constant directive to Christian engagement: *"May all the faithful unceasingly pour out prayers to the Mother of God and the Mother of men, so that She, who with her prayers helped the first fruits of the Church, now may also intercede with her Son in Heaven, so that all the families of peoples, both those who are called Christian and those still ignorant of their savior, may be happily reunited in peace and harmony, in a single people of God, to the glory of the most holy and indivisible Trinity."*

The present era requires that the Church be a *missionary community* and that each individual Christian feel responsible for the salvation of the world.

May the Most Holy Virgin enlighten you always, sustain you in your undertakings, and comfort you as you carry out the pastoral plans of the individual diocese.

OCTOBER 10, 1986

To the Marian Movements

O Mother of the Church!
Help us rediscover
all the simplicity and dignity
of the Christian vocation!
Let there be no shortage of
workers
in the vineyard of the Lord.
Sanctify families!
Watch over the spirits of the
young
and the hearts of children...

JUNE 4, 1979

Mary prays for us and with us

"She was greatly troubled at the saying, and considered in her mind what sort of greeting this might be..."

The evangelist Luke says that Mary "was greatly troubled" at the words of the Angel Gabriel, addressed to her at the moment of the Annunciation, and *"considered in her mind what sort of greeting this might be."*

This meditation of Mary's constitutes the first model for the prayer of the Rosary. It is the prayer of those who hold dear the angel's greeting to Mary. People who recite the Rosary take up Mary's meditation in their thoughts and their hearts, and as they recite they ponder *"what sort of greeting this might be."*

First of all they repeat the words addressed to Mary by God himself, through his messenger.

Those who hold dear the angel's greeting to Mary repeat the words that come from God. In reciting the Rosary, we say these words many times. This is not a simplistic repetition. The words addressed to Mary by God himself and uttered by the divine messenger have an *inscrutable content.*

"Hail, O favored one, the Lord is with you..." "Blessed are you among women."

This content is closely linked to the mystery of Redemption. The words of the angel's greeting to Mary introduce this mystery, and at the same time find in it their explanation.

The first reading of the daily liturgy expresses it, which brings us to the Book of Genesis. It is there — against the background of man's first and original sin — that God announces *for the first time* the mystery of Redemption. *For the first time* he makes known his action in the future history of man and the world.

Therefore, to the tempter who is concealed in the guise of a serpent, the Creator speaks thus: *"I will put enmity between you and the woman, and between your seed and her seed; he shall bruise your head, and you shall bruise his heel."*

The words that Mary heard at the Annunciation reveal that the time has come for the fulfillment of the promise contained in the Book of Genesis. From the proto-gospel we move to the Gospel. The mystery of Redemption is about to be fulfilled. The message of the eternal God greets the "Woman": this woman is Mary of Nazareth. It greets her regarding the "seed," which she will receive from God himself: *"The Holy Spirit will come upon you, and the power of the Most High will overshadow you…"* *"You will conceive in your womb and bear a son, and you shall call his name Jesus."*

Decisive words — truly. The angel's greeting to Mary constitutes the beginning of the greatest of "God's works" in the history of man and the world. This greeting opens from close up the prospect of Redemption.

It's not surprising that Mary, hearing the words of that greeting, was "troubled." The approach of the living God always inspires a holy fear. Nor is it surprising that Mary wondered *"what sort of greeting this might be."* The words of the angel placed her in front of an inscrutable divine mystery. Furthermore, they brought her into the orbit of that mystery. One cannot simply take note of the mystery. It must be meditated on again and again, and ever more profoundly. It is powerful enough to fill not only life but eternity.

And let all of us who hold dear the angel's greeting try to participate in Mary's meditation. Let us try to do it above all when we recite the Rosary.

In the words uttered by the messenger to Nazareth, Mary almost glimpses, in God, all her life on earth and its eternity.

Why, hearing that she is to become the Mother of the Son of God, does she respond not with spiritual transport but first of all with the humble *"fiat"*: "Behold, I am the handmaid of the Lord; let it be to me according to your word"?

Is it not perhaps because already at that moment she felt the piercing sorrow of the reign on the throne of David that was to be Jesus'?

At the same time the angel announces that "his kingdom will have no end."

The words of the angel's greeting to Mary begin to reveal all the Mysteries, in which the Redemption of the world will be fulfilled: the Joyful Mysteries, the Sorrowful, the Glorious. Just as in the Rosary.

Mary, who *"considered in her mind what sort of greeting this might be,"* seems to enter into all these mysteries, introducing us into them, too.

She introduces us into the mysteries of Christ and at the same time to our own mysteries. Her act of meditation at the moment of the Annunciation opens up the pathways to our meditations during the recitation of the Rosary and as a result of it.

The Rosary is the prayer through which, by repeating the angel's greeting to Mary, we seek to draw from the meditation of the Most Holy Virgin our own thoughts on the mystery of

Redemption. This reflection of hers—begun at the *moment* of the Annunciation—continues into the glory of the Assumption. In eternity, Mary, deeply immersed in the Mystery of the Father, the Son, and the Holy Spirit, *joins* as our Mother the *prayer* of those who hold dear the angel's greeting and express it in the recitation of the Rosary.

In this prayer we are united with her like the Apostles gathered in the Upper Room after the Ascension of Christ. The second reading of the daily liturgy reminds us, as recorded in the Acts of the Apostles. The author—after citing the names of the individual Apostles—writes: *"All these with one accord devoted themselves to prayer, together with the women and Mary the Mother of Jesus, and with his brothers."*

With this prayer they prepared to receive the Holy Spirit, on the day of Pentecost.

Mary, who on the day of the Annunciation had received the Holy Spirit in eminent fullness, prayed with them. The special fullness of the Holy Spirit determines in her a special fullness of prayer as well. Through this singular fullness, Mary prays for us—and she prays with us.

She presides over our prayer like a mother. She brings together throughout the world the vast crowds of those who cherish the angel's greeting: they, with her, "meditate on" the Mystery of the Redemption of the world, by reciting the Rosary.

Thus the Church is continuously preparing to receive the Holy Spirit, as on the day of Pentecost.

This year is the first centenary of Pope Leo XIII's Encyclical *Supremi apostolatus,* in which the great Pope decreed that the month of October should be specially devoted to the worship of the Virgin of the Rosary. In this document, he emphasized insistently the extraordinary effectiveness which that prayer, recited with a pure and devout heart, has in obtaining from the Heavenly Father, in Christ, and through the intercession of the Mother of God, protection against the most dangerous evils that threaten Christianity and humanity itself, and in achieving the great goods of justice and peace among individuals and peoples.

With this historic gesture, Leo XIII did no more than align himself with the numerous Popes who preceded him — among them Saint Pius V — and left a legacy for those who would follow him in promoting the practice of the Rosary. For this reason, I, too, wish to say to all of you: make the Rosary the *"sweet chain that unites you to God"* by means of Mary.

I am overjoyed at being able to celebrate with you today the solemn liturgy of the Queen of the Holy Rosary. In this meaningful way we all involve ourselves in the extraordinary Jubilee of the year of Redemption.

All together let us address the Mother of God affectionately, repeating the words of the Angel Gabriel: *"Hail, O favored one, the Lord is with you…" "Blessed are you among women."*

And at the center of today's liturgy let us listen to Mary's response:

> *"My soul magnifies the Lord,*
> *and my spirit rejoices in God my Savior,*
> *for he has regarded the low estate of his handmaiden.*
> *For behold, henceforth all generations*
> *will call me blessed."*

OCTOBER 2, 1983

The Rosary is a true conversation with Mary

Never tire of knowing the Mother of God better and better, and above all do not tire of imitating her in her complete openness to the will of God; occupy yourselves solely with pleasing her, so that you will never make her sad.

You know it's essential to pray, and you would like to do so by recalling and considering what Jesus has done and suffered for us: the Mysteries of his infancy, of his Passion and Death, of his glorious Resurrection.

Reciting your "Mystery," or "decade," you follow the inspiration of the Holy Spirit, who, instructing you from within, leads you to imitate Jesus more closely by making you pray with Mary and, above all, like Mary. The Rosary is a great contemplative prayer, just as useful to the men and women of today, "all busy with many things"; it is the prayer of Mary and those who are devoted to her.

The Mysteries of the Rosary are justly compared to windows that you can push open and then let your gaze sink into the "world of God." It is only from that world, from the "example that Jesus left us," that you learn to be strong in trouble, patient in adversity, resolute in temptation.

You are organized into groups of fifteen, according to the number of the Mysteries of the Rosary, and you pray for one another. And so, while all of you together offer the Mother of the Redeemer the whole Crown of Hail Marys, you more easily fulfill the Word of the Lord: *"For where two or three are gathered in my name, there am I in the midst of them."*

The certainty of having Jesus with you, while you meditate on the Rosary, should make you fervent in praying to him for peace and justice for the Church and for the world, through the intercession of Our Lady.

The founder of your association, Paolina Jaricot, suggests this to you, reminding you that faith can be gained only through prayer.

But above all the Mother of the Lord suggests this to you, she who at Lourdes and especially at Fatima as a mother invited you to recite the Holy Rosary devoutly every day.

The Pope, too, encourages you in this daily recitation, for he, as you know, has made the Rosary "his favorite prayer." He encourages you above all to make yours the virtues that you recognize in the Mysteries of the Holy Rosary. Say this prayer with your friends and recite it especially in your family with the appropriate enthusiasm and persistence.

The Rosary is a true conversation with Mary, our Heavenly Mother. In the Rosary we speak to Mary so that she may intercede for us with her Son Jesus. Thus we speak to God through Mary.

Dear boys and girls, you should get used to reciting the Rosary this way. It is not so much a matter of repeating formulas; rather, it is to speak as living persons with a living person, who, if you do not see her with the eyes of your body, you may, however, see with the eyes of faith. Our Lady, in fact, and her Son Jesus, live in Heaven a life much more "alive" than the mortal one that we live here on earth.

The Rosary is a confidential conversation with Mary, in which we speak to her freely and trustingly. We confide in her our troubles, reveal to her our hopes, open our hearts to her. We declare that we are at her disposal for whatever she, in the name of her Son, may ask of us. We promise faithfulness to her in every circumstance, even the most painful and difficult, sure of her protection, sure that if we ask she will obtain from her Son all the grace necessary for our salvation.

May the Holy Virgin watch over you always, dear boys and girls. May she guard you on your path, in your Christian and human development.

So, too, may she protect your parents, teachers, relatives, friends.

May she bless generously, too, the Brothers and Sisters of the ancient and glorious order of St. Dominic, who originated this devotion of the Rosary, which today is spread throughout the Church.

APRIL 25, 1987

The world needs your goodness

Dear boys and girls,

You belong to that special association of prayer and the Apostolate that is called the Armata Bianca, because it is consecrated to Most Holy Mary.

You have come from many cities of Italy accompanied by some of your bishops, to whom I address my brotherly greeting, grateful to them as I am to all of you. My greeting goes, too, to those who arranged this meeting, to your families and the organizers of this trip. Above all I thank the Lord, who has given you a great faith that is simple, but fervent and profound: *"Let the children come to me, and do not hinder them; for to such belongs the Kingdom of God."*

You are aware of the responsibilities of your organization: devotion to God the Father and to Mary, a commitment to reciting the Rosary, with the particular aims of reparation and of praying for the conversion of many to the Christian message.

I urge you to be faithful to that task, adding to your prayers the testimony of goodness. The world needs your goodness and your innocence in order to rediscover the path of Christ and find the way out of so many situations of moral poverty. Dear children, proclaim the value of goodness through the power of your generosity and grace, through a strong, generous friendship with Jesus Christ. Mankind today feels an immense need for such a message, perhaps even a great nostalgia, an impelling desire. Therefore, be faithful to your commitment of prayer and devotion to Most Holy Mary. You are well aware that the message and the invitation of the Virgin to the children of Fatima is essentially this: *"Pray, pray intensely, and make sacrifices for the sinners."*

I, too, would like to leave you with a souvenir of this visit, and I do so in the form of a suggestion: Be faithful to your meetings with Eucharistic Jesus, joyfully taking part in Mass on Sundays and holidays. Jesus calls you together for holidays, he wants you near him during his sacrifice; he wishes to be in communion with you.

From Jesus you learn to love your neighbor, to be generous toward all, to look for moments of solidarity with those who suffer, with those who need you.

Help the Church in her mission as Teacher of truth, Mother of grace. Help her also to spread the faith. You can do that by studying the Catechism, by knowing its content, and by your affectionate response to the calls of the bishops and priests who guide you.

May you be powerful apostles of Jesus for your friends, and frequently say for them the prayer taught by the children of Fatima:

> *"My God,*
> *I believe, adore, hope and love you!*
> *I ask you for forgiveness*
> *for those who do not believe,*
> *do not adore you, do not have hope in you,*
> *and do not love you."*

May the Virgin Mary protect you, watch over you, enable you to persevere in the firm determination to recite the Rosary.

MAY 27, 1989

Armata Bianca is an international movement of children, twelve and younger, which seeks to reach out to children to consecrate them to God through the Immaculate Heart of Mary, to teach them to pray and do penance, and to help them realize how truly powerful their prayers are before God the Father.

I invite all those who are listening to me at this moment to join with me in this prayer, "so simple, yet so rich," in which we are urged to meditate on the principal episodes of the mystery of salvation as it was fulfilled in Christ: his birth and infancy; his Passion and Death; his Resurrection and Ascension; the descent of the Holy Spirit on the infant Church, and the glorification of his most pure and beloved Mother.

On October 29, 1978, a few days after my election to the Supreme Pontificate, I exhorted the faithful gathered in St. Peter's Square this way: *"The Rosary is my favorite prayer. It is a marvelous prayer! Marvelous in its simplicity and in its profundity. In this prayer we repeat over and over again the words that were spoken to the Virgin Mary by the angel and by her kinswoman Elizabeth. The entire Church shares in these words. One might say that the Rosary is, in a certain sense, a comment-prayer on the last chapter of the Constitution* Lumen Gentium *of the Second Vatican Council, a chapter that treats of the miraculous presence of the Mother of God in the mystery of Christ and the Church."*

To her, to her Immaculate Heart, I entrust you, your loved ones, Italy, the Church, all humanity, so that justice and peace may flourish.

OCTOBER 6, 1984

Loving and serving Christ among your brothers

What a comfort it is for me to know that you, and so many others like you, pray and offer sorrows and sufferings to strengthen my apostolic ministry. The Redemption had its climax in the Passion, Death, and Resurrection of Jesus. Every commitment to realize its efficacy reaches a peak in the offering of the suffering of each one, in loving communion with Christ who died and is risen.

May each of you live every instant of your own existence in this luminous perspective, taking from it a constantly renewed incentive to love and serve Christ among his brothers. I am near you with great affection, and I bless you, those who have been present at the Work and those who do all that they can for you with holy generosity and an evangelical spirit.

SEPTEMBER 3, 1983

Persevere in your devotion to the Virgin

Dear brothers and sisters, persevere in your devotion to the Most Holy Virgin, letting her guide you in every aspect of your life. Listen to this incomparable Teacher, who speaks to you of Jesus in particular through the *Mysteries of the Rosary,* an evocative and effective synthesis of the entire Gospel. Recite the *crown* — the complete Rosary — with simplicity and fervor, to obtain the *joy* of a duty performed, the strength to face the inevitable *pain* of our human condition, the courage that is reborn every day in contemplation of the *glory* promised by God to his faithful servants.

OCTOBER 1, 1983

I urge on you the prayer of the Rosary,
in which, as Paul VI taught
in the Apostolic Exhortation
Marialis cultus,
by contemplating the principal events of salvation
that were fulfilled in Christ,
we see the way in which the Word of God,
mercifully entering
into human affairs,
brought about the Redemption.

FEBRUARY 17, 1983

A *month dedicated to Mary*

Let us entrust our prayer
to the most Holy Virgin,
Queen of Peace.
The month of October,
which begins today,
is dedicated to her.
Let us not fail
to invoke her every day
with the beautiful prayer of the Rosary.
Her heavenly aid
will make the work of each of us valuable
in the service of peace.

OCTOBER 1, 1989

Today the month of May begins. According to a great Catholic tradition, it is dedicated to the Mother of God, Mary. We see before us, adorned with flowers and candles, her image as the mother of believers, as the protector of peoples, as the Queen of Peace.

> *Help us,*
> *Mary, the time has come,*
> *help us, merciful mother!*

Trustfully, we pray to Mary, whom Jesus on the Cross gave us as our mother.

> *Help us,*
> *merciful mother.*

How many times in the past have your bishops, priests, and brothers prayed in this way, in times of trouble, before the suffering image of Our Lady.

We, too, entrust ourselves with filial love to the Mother of Our Lord. He who puts himself in the hands of Mary, who lets himself be led by her, is well guided; he finds the path of faith, the path that Mary, our model, traveled before him; he is ready for the message of Christ, her Son is our brother; he is never alone, in suffering or in death. Faithful and resolute, he can fulfill his earthly duties and set out on the path of the future. For him and for all Christians this future lies in God. Thank him and praise him. Amen.

MAY 1, 1987

The feast of the Blessed Virgin of the Holy Rosary, who is specially venerated in the Sanctuary of Pompeii, offers us a *simple yet profound prayer*, suitable for intensifying this intimate communion with Mary, who is the source of generous dedication to the work of her Son, Jesus.

It is the *Holy Rosary*. It offers us a summary of the Gospel and, in a way that is easy and accessible to all, leads us to a prayer from our hearts.

OCTOBER 6, 1991

In the Marian month of October, I wish to remind you all of the pious practice of the Holy Rosary. Whether you are alone or in the family, in the parish or in the community, may this prayer always carry you to the heart of the mysteries of Christ, our Redeemer, and to the heart of his Most Holy Mother.

OCTOBER 9, 1991

Today is the commemoration of the Mother of the Holy Rosary. The entire month of October is the month of the Rosary. Now that, after an absence of almost five months, I am able to meet with you again, dear brothers and sisters, in the Wednesday audience, I want these first words that I address to you to be words of gratitude, love, and deep trust. Just as the Holy Rosary is and always will be a prayer of gratitude, love, and trustful supplication: the prayer of the Mother of the Church.

And to this prayer I encourage and invite all of you, yet again, especially during this month of the Rosary.

OCTOBER 7, 1981

We invoke Mary on the road of life

Today is the first Sunday of October, when we venerate Our Lady of the Holy Rosary and traditionally call on her with this beautiful prayer, so dear to the faithful. It is therefore a pleasure to have the occasion to urge you to the daily recitation of the Rosary, which—as Paul VI, of sainted memory, wrote in the Apostolic Exhortation *Marialis Cultus*—"is a Gospel prayer, centered on the Mystery of the Redemptive Incarnation . . . a prayer that is clearly oriented to Christ." The recitation of both the Angelus and the Rosary should be a spiritual oasis in the course of the day for every Christian and even more for Christian families, so that they may renew their trust and courage.

OCTOBER 5, 1980

Queen of the Rosary, our beloved Mother

I invite you all to join spiritually in this chorus of prayer and to follow the last part of the "Petition," which I am now about to recite:

> O blessed Rosary of Mary,
> sweet chain that unites us to God,
> chain of love that unites us to the angels.
> Tower of salvation against the assaults of hell.
> Safe harbor in the universal shipwreck,
> we will never abandon you.
> You will be our comfort in the hour of death,
> to you the last kiss
> of our dying life.
> And the final word on our lips
> will be your sweet name,
> O Queen of the Rosary of Pompeii,
> O dearest Mother,
> O refuge of sinners,
> O sovereign comforter of the afflicted.
> Be everywhere blessed, today and forever,
> on earth and in Heaven.
> *Amen.*

MAY 8, 1983

I invite you to say the Hail Mary often

The expression *"Kaíre,"* usually translated as "Ave," or "Hail," properly means "Rejoice," and echoes the announcements of messianic joy addressed by the prophets to the "Daughter of Zion," to assure her of the coming of the Lord among his people. The Angel Gabriel announces the fulfillment of the promise to Mary, the true Daughter of Zion, revealing that the new presence of the Savior among the people will acquire in her the dimension of a real human being. *Full of grace* is the new name given to her by God himself, and means that Mary is and will permanently be the object of divine favor, and that she has a special vocation in the history of salvation. All her other privileges arise from the reality expressed by the name of grace, which indicates her singularity.

The words of the angel were the first hymn addressed to the Heavenly Queen, in the name of all the bands of angels, and the sons of men then wished to enrich the words by making them the preeminent Marian prayer.

I call on all of you to recite the Hail Mary frequently during the day, in the desire to reach the water at the wellspring of the true life.

NOVEMBER 8, 1987

Blessed is she who believed

"Blessed is she who believed."

These words, addressed to Mary by Elizabeth during the Visitation, *go to the heart of our prayer of the Rosary.*

Especially in this month of October, which is the month of the Rosary.

We recite the individual decades, we meditate on the Mysteries, one after the other—Joyful, Sorrowful, Glorious—and during each one we cry out to Mary as Elizabeth did during the Visitation:

"Blessed is she who believed."

—You who believed with joyous faith: at the Annunciation, at the Visitation, at the Nativity, at the presentation in the temple, at the finding in the temple;

—You who believed with sorrowful faith: during the Passion of Gethsemane, the scourging, the crown of thorns, the Via Crucis; you who believed at the Cross on Calvary;

—You who believed with the faith of coming glory in the glorification of your Son: in the Resurrection, the Ascension, the day of Pentecost. You whose faith was fulfilled in the Assumption: our Mother, decked with the crown of heavenly glory!

Thus we pray to Mary, reciting the Holy Rosary.

OCTOBER 14, 1984

Nothing in your pain is lost

Following the desire of our heavenly Mother, we express our love and our trust in her through the Rosary. And so I urge you all to continue the daily recitation of this marvelous prayer, which is truly helpful in our spiritual life. In fact, the Rosary, with its meditation on the Mysteries, and with its trustful invocation of maternal protection in life and death, comforts us in the commitment to model our Christian life on that of Jesus and Mary; calls on us to imitate them with the help of God's grace; and spurs us to practice all the virtues, especially that of brotherly charity.

The Rosary has immense benefits for every person's spiritual life, for the family environment, and for the social and ecclesial environment of every parish.

Dear faithful, especially those who are sick!

May the Rosary be with you every day so that you may conform to the wishes of Our Lady, as the Saints did!

Together with your friends and relatives, who care for you with loving devotion, I ask for you from the Most Holy Virgin the great gift of health, and the strength to resign yourselves to the will of God.

May Jesus, who says, *"Come unto me, all you who are heavy laden and oppressed, and I will give you rest,"* be a source of comfort and support: abandon yourselves to him with total trust, certain that he will miss none of your pain. If your faith in Christ and in the reality of his presence in those who suffer is deeply rooted, your courage will never fail! We will understand in Heaven

the value of human suffering in the plan of Providence for bringing to fulfillment the "story of salvation."

Finally, I wish to entrust to your prayer and your intentions
all the needs of the Church. Your Apostolate of prayer and
suffering is surely indispensable for the good of the Church:
you, too, are in the front lines of support in the work of evangelization, conversion, and sanctification in the world.

Dear sick ones! I entrust to you the job of praying for the
Church, for the Pope, for priestly and religious vocations.

SEPTEMBER 6, 1986

The Mysteries

The Rosary
is a prayer deeply cherished
in Marian piety.
It is a popular form
that we, as children, address to Our Lady,
"Janua caeli," the gate of Heaven.
Turning to her,
as if in familiar conversation,
with our repeated invocation,
we can be introduced
to the contemplation of the Mysteries,
that is, pictures from the story
of our salvation,
meditated on in the light of her presence;
it is she who enables us to look upon
the great scenes of the life of Jesus
as if they were superimposed
on the humble doings of our own existence.
It is a kind of spiritual television.

Offering of the Holy Rosary

Once again
we want to honor you,
most favored Mother of Jesus,
for the light that shines from you
by virtue of the Resurrection of the Lord.

And with our humble filial homage
we intend to redress
the offenses that are made against you,
wishing to exalt
the dignity and purity
of your Immaculate Conception.

To you we entrust
the joy we feel in being Christians,
eager in trust and love
for the firstborn, the Redeemer of humanity,
Jesus your Son and our divine brother.

A pledge of love to the Mother of God

In the Joyful Mysteries, we learn from the examples of Our Lady, who kept all the memories of her Son in her heart, to devote ourselves to God and serve him alone, and we are compelled to carry out the divine will generously, to love our neighbor, and help him in his needs; we are encouraged not to complain in the difficulties that life may present to us, remembering that for us Jesus became poor and hidden. In the school of the "living Rosary," we learn to join sacrifice to prayer: there we are taught to concern ourselves mainly with the matters that concern the Lord, and in the Sorrowful Mysteries we learn that it is impossible to be a true Christian, and aim for perfection, without spiritually climbing Calvary with Jesus and Mary, and meekly accepting suffering and the crosses that the Lord allows us to bear. To succeed in this noble undertaking we must fight sin ceaselessly, and continuously purify our souls of all the sins we have committed. Finally, through meditating on the Glorious Mysteries we can be united with the risen Christ, ardent in our hearts and purified of every stain of sin, so that we may carry out his will forever, in expectation of praising him for all eternity.

Reciting the Rosary in this way, we will advance in virtue and be increasingly fervent, knowing that we are in the school of holiness.

A goal of your movement is to pray for the good of the Church, the Mystical Body of Jesus, as the Second Vatican Council said: *"This is the purpose of the Church: to make all men, through the spreading of the Kingdom of Christ on earth to the glory of God the*

Father, share in the salvation brought about by Redemption, and through them in turn to orient the whole world to Christ. All the activity of the Mystical Body organized to this end is called the 'Apostolate,' which the Church exercises through all its members, naturally in different ways; the Christian vocation is in fact by its nature a vocation also to the Apostolate." Make your lives, therefore, a generous gift of Apostolate, an effort to win over others; pray, too, for the conversion of those who are, unfortunately, far from the grace of God, and petition Our Lady that she may obtain for the Church itself from her divine Son these great goals.

We ask that through your faith in the bosom of your families, and among your contemporaries, you spread this form of prayer. The Pope exhorts you to do so by the force of example and also with that persistence which is proper to your age. Jesus is with you, Our Lady is with you; they will hear you and insure peace in your families and in the world.

MAY 7, 1981

The Joyful Mysteries

Mother of Christ and Mother of the Church,
we entrust and consecrate to you
the bishops, the clergy, the men and women religious,
the contemplative monks and nuns,
the seminarians, the novices.
We entrust and consecrate to you
fathers and mothers, youths and children,
husbands and wives and those who are preparing for
marriage,
those who are called to serve
you and their neighbor in celibacy.
Help us all to work together
with a sense of the Christian ideal
and for a common Christian goal.
Help us persevere with Christ;
help us, O Mother of the Church,
to construct his Mystical Body,
by living that life which he alone
can grant us from his fullness,
which is both human and divine.

SEPTEMBER 30, 1979

The Rosary elevates our feelings

The Holy Rosary is a Christian, Gospel, and ecclesial prayer, but it is also a prayer that elevates our feelings and affections.

In the Joyful Mysteries, on which we dwell briefly today, we see some of this: joy in the family, in maternity, in kinship, in friendship, in mutual aid. These are joys that sin has not annihilated, and Christ made man took them into himself and sanctified them. He achieved this through Mary. So it is through her that, even today, we can grasp the joys of man and make them our own: in themselves they are humble and simple, but in Mary and Jesus they become great and holy.

In Mary, who as a virgin was married to Joseph and who conceived by divine means, there is the joy of the chaste love of spouses and of maternity received and protected as a gift of God; in Mary, who eagerly goes to Elizabeth, there is the joy of serving our brothers by bringing to them the presence of God; in Mary, who presents to the shepherds and the Magi the long-awaited one of Israel, there is the spontaneous and trustful sharing of friendship; in Mary, who in the temple offers her own Son to the Heavenly Father, there is the anxious joy of parents and teachers for their children or students; in Mary, who after three days of anguished searching, finds Jesus, there is the painful joy of the mother who knows that her Son belongs to God before he belongs to her.

OCTOBER 23, 1983

The Christian is the man of the Annunciation

With the prayer of the Rosary, we try to extend our gaze, in faith, to all the Mysteries that have as their source the Annunciation: the Joyful Mysteries of the Incarnation, the Sorrowful Mysteries of the sacrifice on the Cross, the Glorious Mysteries of the Resurrection.

Thus, in a simple and humble way, we all wish to follow the model of the "Handmaid of the Lord."

We hold in the depths of our hearts the whole divine mystery of our vocation in Christ.

With Mary, we desire, each of us and all together, to become "men and women of the Annunciation."

OCTOBER 7, 1986

Mary, mother in the order of grace

Dear brothers and sisters!

The time has come to recite the Angelus, the prayer that every day recalls to us the Mystery of the Incarnation of the Word of God in the womb of Most Holy Mary.

Today, at the festival of the Trinity, the liturgical celebration asks us to recall in a special spirit of faith the fact that at the Annunciation, Mary was introduced in a special way to the mystery of revelation and the Trinitarian life. The angel announces to Mary that the Lord is with her, because God has filled her with grace, with the fullness of the gift of divine life. Along with that greeting the work of the Holy Spirit is revealed to her, he who will come upon her and overshadow her.

At the Annunciation, Mary grasps the Mystery of the Incarnation of the Son of God: he who will be born to her is the Word of God, and in her is made flesh. In the salvific sign of the Most Holy Trinity the gift of the Incarnation constitutes the apex and the center of the revelation of himself that God made to man, and the apex of the gift that God makes of himself and his life for our salvation. In Christ, in fact, God said to us the defining word of his truth: *"All that I have heard from my Father I have made known to you"*; and in Christ the promise of Redemption is fulfilled.

Communicating this mystery of the One and Triune God, Mary becomes the instrument of grace, destined to bring salvation, through the action of Jesus, to all humanity. Grace, which has its source in the life of the Trinity, is given fully to Mary, and by virtue of this privilege Mary became "our mother in the order of grace."

MAY 21, 1989

Remember the source of grace

Let us recite the Angelus Domini, a prayer that is traditional and familiar, which the ringing of your parish bells invites you to every day, echoing from valley to valley. The Angelus Domini is one of the most beautiful and comprehensive prayers of devotion to Mary: in it we contemplate God's plan of salvation and his merciful love for all creation, a plan that is fulfilled in the choice of Mary to become the mother of the Redeemer.

The Angelus Domini presents the Mother of Jesus to us as the true and exemplary believer, who with her "yes" becomes the model for all believers. This "yes," which Mary said for the first time with complete availability, was repeated again by her in the most difficult situations of her life, as she journeyed all the way to the end of the road of faith.

In the Angelus Domini we gratefully remember the fundamental event in which God came among men: *"And the Word became flesh and dwelt among us, full of grace and truth."* He is truly Emanuel, God with us.

Many pilgrims go to these sanctuaries to invoke God's mercy and honor the Mother of God. Usually, when we return from a pilgrimage, we bring back a souvenir or a sign that recalls it to memory: the prayer of the Angelus Domini could be this sign, which every day reminds us of the source of grace, Jesus Christ, the Son of the Virgin Mary.

JULY 17, 1988

The Sorrowful Mysteries

In Christ we contemplate the sorrows of mankind

With the Sorrowful Mysteries we contemplate in Christ all the sorrows of mankind: in Christ suffering, betrayed, abandoned, captured, imprisoned; in him unjustly accused and placed under the scourge; in him misunderstood and mocked in his mission, in him condemned with the complicity of the political authorities; in him led publicly to execution and exposed to a humiliating death; in him — the Man of sorrow predicted by Isaiah — is summed up and sanctified every human sorrow.

Servant of the Father, Firstborn among many brothers, the Head of humanity, he transforms man's suffering into an offering that pleases God, a redeeming sacrifice. He is the Lamb who takes away the sins of the world, the faithful Witness who recapitulates in himself every martyrdom and ennobles it.

On the Via Dolorosa and on Golgotha is his Mother, the first Martyr. And with the heart of his Mother, to whom he consigned as his testament from the Cross every disciple and every man, we contemplate, with emotion, Christ's sufferings, learning from him obedience until death, even death on the Cross; learning from her to accept every man as our brother, to be with her near the innumerable crosses to which the Lord of glory is still unjustly nailed, not his glorious Body but the suffering limbs of his mystical Body.

OCTOBER 30, 1983

The agony of Jesus in the garden of Gethsemane

In these Sunday meetings of ours for Marian prayer during Lent, as we journey toward Easter, we would like to pause and reflect on the Sorrowful Mysteries of the Holy Rosary. Accompanying us in our reflections is the Virgin Mary, who was an eyewitness of the culminating moment of the Passion.

We speak of *mysteries,* because they are at once *events* in the story of Jesus and *events* of our salvation. They are a *road* that Jesus traveled and travels with us so that we may experience, through conversion, communion with God and renewed brotherhood with mankind.

Today we meditate on the first Sorrowful Mystery: the agony of Jesus in the garden of Gethsemane. The evangelist and teacher of this liturgical year, St. Luke, guides us. He reports that Jesus, coming from the Last Supper, went "as usual" to the Mount of Olives. He was not alone; his Disciples, though they didn't understand, followed him. Twice, at the beginning and at the end of the event, he addressed to them the exhortation that we utter daily in the Our Father: *"Pray that you may not enter into temptation."*

This Sunday and for the next week of Lent, we welcome this divine word as a viaticum and as a genuine reminder: *"Pray that you may not enter into temptation."*

During the final trial of his life, Jesus prays in solitude: *"And he withdrew from them about a stone's throw, and knelt down and prayed."*

The content of the prayer is filial, extended into Jesus' inner agony to accept the will of the Father, faithful even in anguish for what is about to happen: *"Father, if thou art willing, remove this cup from me; nevertheless not my will, but thine, be done."*

And Jesus begins to suffer in a way that dramatically involves his whole person: *"His sweat was like drops of blood falling to the ground."* But his prayer became *"more fervent."*

Brothers and sisters, we contemplate Jesus in physical pain, in harrowing psychological and moral pain, in his abandonment and solitude, but *in prayer,* in the effort to adhere to the Father in total faithfulness.

In this season of Lent we have a precise task: *to interpret our suffering in the light of the suffering of Jesus* — experienced in grief and compassion — and to pray, to pray more and more.

Prayer in the privacy of our room; prayer in offering our work; prayer in listening to and meditating on the Word of God; prayer in the family through the Holy Rosary; liturgical prayer, the source and culmination of our inner life.

Most Holy Mary teaches us both to accept suffering in an attitude of obedient love and to elevate our soul to God through daily prayer. Especially during this time of Lent, we want to enroll ourselves, as attentive disciples, in her school.

FEBRUARY 12, 1989

Jesus is scourged

In the Marian prayer of the second Sunday of Lent, let us reflect on the second sorrowful mystery of the Rosary: Jesus is scourged.

The Gospel of St. Luke emphasizes three times the tortures that Jesus suffered before he was put to death.

First of all, before his appearance at the Sanhedrin: *"Now the men who were holding Jesus mocked him and beat him; they also blindfolded him and asked him, 'Prophesy! Who is it that struck you?' And they spoke many other words against him, reviling him."* He who more than any-one else deserved to be called *prophet* — that is, one who speaks in the name and with the power of God — is mocked because of what for him is the most profound personal reality: being the Word of God.

An analogous scene is repeated in the encounter with Herod Antipas: *"And Herod with his soldiers treated him with contempt and mocked him; then, arraying him in gorgeous apparel, he sent him back to Pilate."*

And when Jesus comes before Pilate, Luke notes, for the third time: *"Pilate said: ... I will therefore chastise him and release him."*

St. Mark describes this punishment: "So Pilate, wishing to satisfy the crowd, released for them Barabbas; and *having scourged Jesus,* he delivered him to be crucified."

The Roman *flagellatio,* or scourging, carried out by soldiers equipped with the *flagellum,* or *flagrum,* a whip made of knotted leather cords, or bearing at the end a blunt instrument, was the punishment reserved for slaves and those condemned to death.

Its effects were terrible: those upon whom it was inflicted often died under the lashes.

Jesus would not spare himself even this horrific suffering: he confronted it for us.

Meditating on this second sorrowful mystery of the Rosary, we hear ourselves called to be disciples of Jesus in his suffering. He prayed for us also with *his body*, subjecting it to unspeakable tortures in obedience to the plan of the Father. He gave himself to the Father and to men, manifesting to all of us unfathomable human misery and the extraordinary possibility of renewal and salvation, which is given to us in him.

On the example of Jesus, we, too, must pray with our bodies. The choices that require demanding and difficult behavior, such as chastity according to one's state of life, giving assistance to our brothers and sisters, and other physically tiring activities, become prayer and sacrifice to be offered to God in a redemptive union with the "sufferings of Christ."

We therefore accept the "scourge" that personal sobriety and the exercise of Christian charity, every day, make us experience. It is the fruit and gift of the sorrowful mystery of Jesus, which spurs us on, involves us, transforms us inwardly.

May the Virgin of Sorrows lighten our task with her intercession.

FEBRUARY 19, 1989

Jesus is crowned with thorns

Let us devote today's meeting for the Marian prayer to the contemplation of the third sorrowful mystery: the crowning of Jesus with thorns.

The moment is attested to by the Gospels, which, though they do not dwell on many details, point out the acts of aggression and the insane enjoyment of Pilate's soldiers.

"And the soldiers," Mark writes, followed by Matthew and John, *"led him away inside the palace (that is, the praetorium); and they called together the whole battalion. And they clothed him in a purple cloak, and plaiting a crown of thorns they put it on him. And they began to salute him, 'Hail, King of the Jews!' And they struck his head with a reed, and spat upon him, and they knelt down in homage to him."*

Matthew adds only one detail: a mocking symbol of royalty: first they place the reed in Jesus' right hand, like a royal scepter, then they take it away from him and beat him on the head with it.

We have before us an image of sorrow, which evokes all the homicidal madness, all the sadism of history. Jesus, too, wanted to be at the mercy of the sometimes extraordinarily cruel wickedness of men.

John induces us to transform our contemplation into worshipful and anxious prayer before the suffering of Jesus crowned with thorns: *"Pilate,"* he writes, *"went out again, and said to them, 'See, I am bringing him out to you, that you may know that I find no crime in him.' So Jesus came out, wearing the crown of thorns and the purple robe. Pilate said to them, 'Behold the man!'"*

Truly that Man is the Son of God, who, through unspeakable suffering, brings to fulfillment the Father's plan of salvation. He has grasped our sorrows so deeply that he shares them, assumes them, gives them meaning, transforms them into an unhoped-for possibility of life, grace, and communion with God and hence glory.

From that day, every human generation has been called to declare itself before that "man" crowned with thorns. No one can remain neutral. One must declare oneself. And not only with words but with one's life.

The Christian accepts the crown of thorns on his head, when he knows how to mortify his arrogance, his pride, the various forms of selfishness and hedonism, which end up destroying him as a person and often lead him to be cruel to others.

Lent invites each of us to enter on the path of liberation from whatever slavery torments us. Our King, the Man-God, is before us: he gives us new heart, so that we may experience our anxiety and our suffering in a form that leads to salvation, through his love and love of our brothers.

The Most Holy Virgin precedes us on this difficult path and encourages us to quicken our steps, pointing out to us the radiant goal of Easter.

FEBRUARY 26, 1989

Jesus on the road to Calvary

In our Lent meeting for the Marian prayer of the Angelus our thoughts turn to the fourth sorrowful mystery of the Holy Rosary: Jesus on the road to Calvary.

Our meditation will emphasize in particular the fact that determined that anguished journey: Jesus' condemnation to death. St. Luke writes: *"The chief priests, the rulers and the people... demanded that he be crucified...he [Pilate] delivered up Jesus to their will."*

"Hand over," "deliver," "handed over" are terms that recur in the story. They are translations of the Latin *tradere* and *traditum,* words that reflect both Pilate's act of cowardice and the plan of the Father and the loving will of the Son, who accepts "being delivered up" for the salvation of the world.

Along the Via Dolorosa the evangelist St. Luke offers us, then, models that teach us to live, in our daily life, the Passion of Jesus as the road to Resurrection.

The first example is Simon of Cyrene, *"who was coming in from the country, and [they] laid on him the cross, to carry it behind Jesus."* It is not only carrying the Cross that is relevant. Many individuals in the world suffer terribly: every people, every family has sorrows and burdens to bear. What gives fullness of meaning to the Cross is that Simon carries it behind Jesus, not on a path of anguished solitude or rebellion but on a path sustained and vivified by the divine presence of the Lord.

The second example consists of the *"great multitude of the people, and of women who bewailed and lamented him [Jesus]."* Compassionate words and even shared tears are not sufficient: we must be cognizant of our own responsibility in the drama of sorrow, especially when it is innocent. That leads us to make a useful contribution to its alleviation.

Jesus' words do not indulge in a sterile sentimentality but invite us to a realistic reading of the history of individuals and communities. *"For if they do this when the wood is green, what will happen when it is dry?"* If the supremely innocent man is abused in this way, what will happen to those who are responsible for the evil that has taken place in the history of individuals and nations?

Jesus' sorrowful journey, the Via Crucis, the Way of the Cross, is a precious reminder to us to recognize the value of our daily suffering; a lesson not to avoid it with opportunistic pretexts or vain excuses; an impetus to make of it instead a gift to him who loved us, in the certainty that in this way we will build a new culture of love and cooperate in the divine work of salvation.

May Mary, who with the other women, followed Jesus on the way of the Cross, and whom we will find on Calvary, be for us a model in this gift of ourselves: may she help us to understand the value of our suffering and offer it to the Father joined with Christ's suffering.

MARCH 5, 1989

Jesus dies on the Cross

On this fifth Sunday of Lent, at the hour of Marian prayer, let us reflect on the fifth sorrowful mystery of the Holy Rosary: Jesus dies on the Cross.

The Crucifixion and Death of Jesus join together Heaven and earth, just as the other fundamental events of the story of salvation do: the creation, the birth of Jesus, the Resurrection, the final coming, or Parousia, of the Lord. The evangelist Luke writes: *"It was now about the sixth hour, and there was darkness over the whole land until the ninth hour, while the sun's light failed."*

This event expresses with stunning clarity how Jesus is a symbol of contradiction. In fact, people line up on two sides: those who know him and adore him; and those who mock him.

St. Luke leads us on to contemplate Jesus in prayer: *"Father, forgive them, for they know not what they do."* It is the most sublime school of love: in sorrow, Jesus tries to forgive those who have made him suffer, responding to evil with good. St. Stephen, the first Christian martyr, will repeat this prayer of Jesus'.

"The rulers" and *"the soldiers,"* disappointed in their expectations, mock Jesus. The people, on the other hand, *"stood by, watching."* The two *"criminals"* also display contradictory attitudes. While one insults him, the other is testimony of an extraordinary experience of reconciliation: he recognizes his own condition as a sinner, which differentiates him radically from the man who is suffering beside him (*"But this man has done nothing wrong"*), and entrusts himself fully to the love of Jesus.

St. John then shows us Mary at the foot of the Cross: a woman of sorrow, which is offered through love; the woman of giving and acceptance; the Mother of Jesus; the Mother of the Church; the Mother of all men.

There were other women, too, near the Cross, but Jesus, *"when he saw his mother, and the disciple whom he loved standing near,"* utters words that have a profound spiritual resonance: *"Woman, behold, your son"; "Behold, your mother."* In John every man discovers that he is the son of the mother who gave to the world the Son of God.

At the moment of death Jesus prays, proclaiming his ultimate *gift* to the Father for the salvation of all men: *"Father, into thy hands I commit my spirit."*

Confronting the mystery of Christ who dies to save us, let us, too, say: *"Truly this man is the Son of God."*

May the Virgin Mary help us in our commitment to the road of faith as we approach the holy days, in worshipful silence, in full willingness to make our life, our particular story, a gift to share, in love and hope, with our brothers.

MARCH 12, 1989

With him, toward life, beyond death

In the preceding notes for the Marian prayer during Lent we considered the Sorrowful Mysteries of the Rosary. This Sunday marks the start of the Holy Week, during which we will relive the various moments of the Passion of Jesus, up to his dramatic and mysterious invocation: *"God my God, why have you forsaken me?,"* just before his last breath. His death—as we all know—was followed by the Resurrection. This week, we, too, with Christ, will make this *"passage"* (Easter).

Today's Angelus marks, in our liturgical program, a sort of point of connection between the period of preparation for the Mysteries of the Passion, Death, and Resurrection of Christ and their celebration. And so today we can look upon the whole spiritual journey that we have made, and the journey that still remains for us. A journey that sums up the entire meaning of Christian life: the life that is born in death. Death, in a certain sense, belongs to the past, while life smiles on us in the future. Let us complete with Christ this Easter, or Passage, which *"is the passage of the Lord."* With him, toward life, beyond death.

MARCH 19, 1989

The Glorious Mysteries

Hail, O Mother, Queen of the World.
You are the Mother of beautiful love,
you are the Mother of Jesus
the source of all grace,
the perfume of every virtue,
the mirror of all purity.
You are joy in distress,
victory in battle,
hope in death.
How sweet the taste
of your name on our lips,
how gentle the harmony
in our ears,
what ecstasy in our hearts!
You are happiness for those who suffer,
the crown of martyrs
the beauty of virgins.
We implore that after this our exile
you will lead us
to possess your Son, Jesus.
Amen.

MAY 1, 1979

Mary is the model of the victorious Church

In the Glorious Mysteries of the Holy Rosary the hopes of the Christian are relived: the hopes of eternal life, which engage God's omnipotence, and the expectations of the present time, which commit men to work with God.

In Christ who rises all the world rises, and there will begin a new Heaven and a new earth, which will be fulfilled at his glorious return, when *"death shall be no more, neither shall there be mourning nor crying nor pain anymore, for the former things have passed away."*

In him who ascends to Heaven human nature is exalted, placed on the right hand of God, and the order to evangelize the world is given to the Disciples; further, in ascending to Heaven, Christ was not taken from the earth: he is concealed in the face of every man and woman, especially the unfortunate: the poor, the ill, the marginalized, the persecuted...

Pouring out the Holy Spirit at Pentecost, he gave the Disciples the strength to love and to spread his truth; he asked for a community that would build a world worthy of man who has been redeemed; and he granted the capacity to sanctify all things in obedience to the will of the Heavenly Father. In this way he rekindled the joy of giving in those who give, and the certainty of being loved in the hearts of the unhappy.

In the glory of the Virgin assumed into Heaven, the first to be redeemed, we contemplate, among other things, the true sublimation of the ties of blood and family affections: Christ glorified Mary not only because she is Immaculate, the ark of the divine presence, but also because, as a Son, he honors his

Mother: the holy bonds of earth do not break in Heaven. Rather, in the solicitude of the Virgin Mother, assumed into Heaven to become our advocate and protector, the model of the victorious Church, we can see the same inspiring example of the attentive love of our beloved dead toward us, not broken by death but made powerful in the light of God.

Finally, in the vision of Mary glorified by all creatures, we celebrate the eschatological mystery of a humanity remade in Christ in perfect unity, with no more divisions, without rivalry, so that one is not ahead of another in love. Because God is Love.

In the Mysteries of the Holy Rosary we contemplate and relive the joys, the sorrows, and the glories of Christ and his Holy Mother, which become the joys, the sorrows, and the hopes of mankind.

NOVEMBER 6, 1983

Fixing our eyes on the Virgin at prayer

Lord Jesus, before miraculously leaving the earth to return to the Father on the day of Ascension, reaffirmed to the eleven Apostles his great promise: *"You shall receive power when the Holy Spirit has come upon you."*

Then they returned quickly to Jerusalem and gathered in the Upper Room. And, in the anxious wait for that event charged with mystery, *"all these with one accord devoted themselves to prayer, together with the women and Mary the Mother of Jesus, and with his brothers."*

This ineffable scene is full of meaning for us today. The Church ideally gathers in the Upper Room to prepare for the new Pentecost, a singular Pentecost, which will coincide with the beginning of the Marian Year.

"Amid the problems, disappointments and hopes, the desertions and returns of these times, the Church remains faithful to the mystery of its birth.... The Church is always in the Upper Room."

In these *"hidden walls"* it hears again, so to speak, its first breath, the first beatings of its heart. And it draws close to Mary, the great spiritual Mother, Mother of all the People of God, of the Pastors as well as of the Faithful.

All of us together, pastors and faithful, keep our eyes fixed on the Virgin in prayer, the gentle life-giving spirit of the early Christian community, destined to spread the light of the Gospel to the farthest ends of the earth to the end of time.

Let us persevere in prayer, allied with her in service to mankind today, knowing that *"these difficult times have a special need for prayer."* In the first place, we need it so that we may have the grace and responsibility to be living members of the ecclesial family, and that we may be called to be credible witnesses to the power of the Holy Spirit, the immense gift given to us to renew everything in Christ.

As we await Pentecost and the start of the Marian Year, the Virgin Mary, the Temple of the Holy Spirit, constantly watches over us with her mother's heart.

MAY 31, 1987

Extend your protection over all the earth

With the simplicity and fervor of St. Bernadette let us recite the Holy Rosary!

First decade:
Let us honor the Resurrection of the Lord Jesus.
— Let us bless the Mother of the victor over death and sin.
—With her, let us bless the risen Christ.
— Let us pray to Mary to strengthen the faith of Christian communities and of the entire world.

Second decade:
Let us honor the exaltation of Christ in the divine glory, the Mystery of the Ascension:
— Let us rejoice with Our Lady at the heavenly glorification of her Son.
— Let us praise Christ, the new Adam, for restoring to men the destiny of immortality and life with God.
— Let us entrust to Mary the individuals and peoples who have lost or who do not know or who fight Christian hope.

Third decade:
Let us celebrate Pentecost.
— Let us praise Mary, in whom the Holy Spirit has given life to the Redeemer of the world.
— Let us praise Jesus who poured out his Spirit on the first Disciples, as he does on those of today.

— Let us entreat Mary, true to the Spirit, to grant this fidelity to the leaders and the members of the Church.

Fourth decade:

Let us honor the Assumption of the Virgin Mary.

— Let us praise Mary of Nazareth, Mary of Bethlehem, of the presentation in the temple, of Cana, of Calvary, of the Upper Room: she was glorified immediately in body and soul.

— Let us thank Jesus for enabling his Mother to share in his life as the Risen one.

— Let us pray to Mary that she may give us the joy and hope of joining her.

Fifth decade:

Let us honor the glorification of Our Lady.

— Let us hail Mary, in keeping with the tradition of the Church, who shares in the spiritual sovereignty of Christ the Redeemer.

— Let us bless Jesus who wished to unite his Mother to the expansion of his Kingdom!

O Mother of the Church,
O Queen of the universe,
we pray to you:
extend over all the earth
your motherly protection!

AUGUST 14, 1983

Tools for Recitation of the Rosary

We are pilgrims in this vale of tears
who sigh to you:
"After this our exile show unto us
the blessed fruit of your womb, Jesus,
O clement, O loving, O sweet Virgin Mary."

FEBRUARY 11, 1980

Mary with the Church
waiting for the gift of the Spirit

(In this example, five events in which the Holy Spirit and the Virgin Mary worked in a particular way are offered for meditation.)

OPENING PRAYER

Let us pray.
Pour into our spirit
your grace, O Father;
you, who in the angel's announcement
revealed to us the Incarnation of your Son,
through his Passion and his Cross
through the intercession of the Blessed Virgin Mary
    guide us
to the glory of the Resurrection.
Through Christ our Lord.
Amen.

Meditation on the Mysteries of the Rosary

First Mystery
THE ANNUNCIATION
The Virgin conceived through the action of the Holy Spirit.

WORD OF THE LORD
From the Gospel according to Luke (1:26–28, 31, 35).

The Angel Gabriel was sent from God to a virgin; and the virgin's name was Mary. And he came to her, and said, "Hail, O favored one, the Lord is with you. Behold, you will conceive in your womb and bear a child. The Holy Spirit will come upon you. The child to be born will be called holy, the Son of God."

—Our Father
— Hail Mary
— Glory Be

Second Mystery
THE VISITATION
Elizabeth, filled with the Holy Spirit,
proclaims that Mary is blessed because of her faith.

WORD OF THE LORD
From the Gospel according to Luke (1:40–42, 45).

Mary entered the house of Zechariah and greeted Elizabeth. And when Elizabeth heard the greeting of Mary, the babe leaped in her womb.

Elizabeth was filled with the Holy Spirit and she exclaimed with a loud cry, "Blessed are you among women, and blessed is the fruit of your womb! And blessed is she who believed that there would be a fulfillment of what was spoken to her from the Lord."

—Our Father
—Hail Mary
—Glory Be

Third Mystery

THE DEATH OF JESUS

From the Cross, in the presence of his mother, Jesus gave up his spirit.

WORD OF THE LORD

From the Gospel according to John (19:26—30).

From the Cross, Jesus said to his mother, "Woman, behold your son!" Then he said to his Disciple: "Behold your mother!"

After this, Jesus, knowing that all was now finished, said (to fulfill the Scripture), "I thirst." Therefore they placed a sponge soaked in vinegar at the top of a reed and brought it to his mouth. And after he took the vinegar, Jesus said, "It is finished." And he bowed his head and gave up his spirit.

—Our Father
—Hail Mary
—Glory Be

Fourth Mystery

THE RESURRECTION

Jesus, through the power of the Spirit, vanquishes death.

WORD OF THE LORD

From the Gospel according to Matthew (28:1–2, 5–6).

Now after the sabbath, toward the dawn of the first day of the week, Mary Magdalene and the other Mary went to see the sepulcher.

And behold, there was a great earthquake; for an angel of the Lord descended from Heaven and came and rolled back the stone, and sat upon it. The angel said to the women: "Do not be afraid, for I know that you seek Jesus who was crucified. He is not here; for he has risen, as he said."

— Our Father
— Hail Mary
— Glory Be

Fifth Mystery

THE PENTECOST

The Spirit descends on Mary and the newborn Church.

WORD OF THE LORD

From the Acts of the Apostles (1:14, 2:1, 3–4).

The Apostles with one accord devoted themselves to prayer, together with the women and Mary, the Mother of Jesus, and with his brothers.

94

When the day of Pentecost had come, there appeared to them tongues as of fire; and they were all filled with the Holy Spirit and began to speak in other tongues as the Spirit gave them utterance.

— Our Father
— Hail Mary
— Glory Be

Meditation

Hail Mary!

With the words of the angel's greeting we have repeatedly invoked in this Rosary the Virgin Mary, the Mother of the Redeemer and our spiritual mother.

Hail Mary! It is a greeting and a prayer. A greeting of praise to she who agreed to cooperate in the birth of the eternal Son of God. A prayer addressed to Almighty God, through the intercession of Her, "full of grace."

Hail Mary! The mystical invocation, alternating with the words of the Our Father and the Glory Be, enables us to experience a moment of profound spiritual communion. A marvelous consonance of hearts echoes on the five continents, in the great temples of Christianity, in innumerable ecclesial and religious communities, in places of suffering and care, in charitable institutions, in many families: a worldwide chorus, of men and women, young and old, all brought together in the language of prayer.

Holy Mary, Mother of God! We have prayed, meditating on the five Mysteries linked to the history of salvation and the presence of Mary.

That meditation has given a breath of incalculable vigor to the words that come from our lips. As we follow the Mysteries of the Rosary, we discover the profound meaning of history, through whose events the Spirit weaves the providential design of salvation. He "pervades man's earthly pilgrimage and makes all creation—all history—flow to its final end, in the infinite ocean of God."

By praying together, we have strengthened the chains of solidarity with the entire human family, in the conviction that the challenges of this difficult time in world history, if they are to be resolved in favor of man and true civilization, must be confronted with a generous opening to the spiritual dimension.

Modern man asks himself, sometimes unconsciously, sometimes with anguish, the meaning of his journey on the pathways of existence. Even in the face of unprecedented progress, the man of today feels profoundly shaken by the contradictions in the world and in people, which lead him sometimes even to doubt the value of life itself. And yet the road to redemption is inscribed in the depths of our hearts. There, where every distracting noise is muted, a voice arrives to enlighten, comfort, fortify: the voice of God, the good and beneficent Father, knowing and providing.

Brothers and sisters scattered from one end of the world to the other, here is the message that the Virgin brings to each of us in this particular moment: God is love!

Whoever you are, whatever your condition of existence, God loves you. He loves you completely. Man is called to communion with his creator. The unquenchable longing for truth and happiness constantly reminds him of this. Man needs God.

Hail Mary! Two thousand years ago these words opened a new chapter in the history of salvation, signifying the "fullness of time." With these very words we express the wish to return to God through Mary. It is she who leads us to Christ.

At the approach of the third millennium of the Incarnation, we would like to fortify our relations with God, as a guarantee of true and good relationships between human beings.

And Mary is the exemplary model of the "new humanity." She is the Woman in whom God's plan is fully realized. At the same time she is the "humble servant of God" and is "full of grace."

Reviewing, through the Mysteries of the Rosary, the stages of Christ's work of salvation, we discover how Mary lived the richest dimension — transcendent yet human — of these events, which left an indelible stamp on humanity's path.

Hail Mary! The sweet prayer echoes joyously in the sacred temples, in the sanctuaries. It marks the footsteps of pilgrims on the roads of time; the footsteps of the People of God on their journey. May the Rosary once again become the daily prayer of that "domestic church" which is the Christian family. The prayer of the Rosary will bring to our world, with the smile of the Virgin Mother, God's words of tender love for mankind, courageous yet fearful, in the twentieth century. This is the hope that surges from our hearts on the threshold of the Marian Year. May that year be a grand Magnificat that the whole Church raises to the Lord, who "gazed on the humbleness of his servant" and brought about in her and for her "great things."

May the Virgin Mary's Magnificat be our Magnificat. Let us

gather up and present to the Father our deepest thanks, because by the action of the Holy Spirit he has given us — through Mary — his beloved Son, our Redeemer, Jesus Christ. To him all honor and glory forever and ever. Amen.

June 6, 1987

Rosary for peace
Prayer, stronger than any weapon

Brothers and sisters,

Our hearts are full of sorrow because of the war going on in the Gulf region, from which day after day news reaches us that is more and more distressing, about the number of combatants and the number of weapons, and the involvement of whole civilian populations.

What makes this even more worrying is the risk that this discouraging picture may extend in both time and space, with tragic and incalculable consequences.

As men and women and as Christians, we must not get used to the idea that this is all unavoidable, and we must not let our souls yield to the temptation of indifference and fatalistic resignation, as if men couldn't help being caught in the spiral of war.

As believers in the God of mercy and in his Son Jesus, who died and rose for the salvation of all, we cannot give up hope that this tremendous suffering, which involves such a large number of people, will end as soon as possible. To achieve this goal, we have at our disposal in the first place prayer, a humble instrument but, if nurtured with sincere and intense faith, stronger than any weapon and any human calculation. We entrust to God our profound sorrow together with our most vivid hope.

Let us call on the divine light for those who, in international spheres, continue to seek ways of peace; who, making efforts to end the war, have a desire for peace and justice, and a strong will to find adequate solutions to the various problems of the Middle East.

We ask the Lord to enlighten the leaders on all sides of the conflict, so that they may find the courage to abandon the road of warlike confrontation, and to trust, sincerely, in negotiation, dialogue, and collaboration.

We ask divine comfort for all those who suffer on account of war and the serious problems of injustice and insecurity that have not yet been solved in the region of the Middle East.

In this trustful appeal to divine mercy, I exhort you all to be in harmony with other believers, above all with the peoples of Jewish, Christian, and Muslim faiths, who are most stricken by this war.

By reciting the Rosary and meditating on the mysteries of Christ, we place our sorrow, our worries, and our hopes in the Immaculate Heart of Mary, our Mother.

FEBRUARY 2, 1991

THEME

The theme of this Rosary is the celebration of some of the principal events in the Story of Salvation, in which what stands out is the design of the Father, who through his Son, Jesus, in the Holy Spirit, wished to communicate to mankind the gift of reconciliation, freedom, and peace.

Together with Mary, the Mother of the Prince of Peace, the protagonist of these events, the Church contemplates the mystery that she celebrates, and, trusting in her maternal intercession, entreats the Father that these days may enjoy the gift of peace, which finds in him its true source.

PRAYER

Let us pray.
O God, who in your only Son
have opened up to men the source of peace,
through the intercession of the blessed Virgin Mary,
give to men and women whom you love
the much desired, long-sought peace,
that they may form a single family
joined in the chain of fraternal charity.
Through Christ our Lord.
Amen.

Meditation on the Mysteries of the Rosary

First Mystery
THE ANNUNCIATION
*In the womb of the Virgin Mary, the Word of God
became man to reconcile man with God.*

WORD OF THE LORD
From the Gospel according to Luke (1:28, 31–33).

The angel came to her and said: "Hail, O favored one, the Lord is with you.... Behold, you will conceive in your womb and bear a son, and you shall call his name Jesus.... The Lord God will give to him the throne of his father David and he will reign over the house of Jacob forever; and of his kingdom there will be no end."

TEACHING OF THE CHURCH
*From the radio message to the world of
Pope Pius XII (August 24, 1939).*

"It is by the force of reason, not of arms, that justice advances. And empires not founded on justice are not blessed by God.... Nothing is lost with peace. Everything can be lost with war. Let men return to understanding one another. Let them begin to negotiate again. If they can negotiate with goodwill and respect for mutual rights, they will realize that sincere, useful dialogue never rules out an honorable conclusion."

—Our Father
—Hail Mary
—Glory Be

PRAYER

Lord,
who are the source of justice and the origin of harmony,
in the angel's announcement to Mary
you brought men the good news
of reconciliation between Heaven and earth:
open men's hearts to dialogue
and support the task of those who work for peace,
so that negotiation will prevail over recourse to arms,
understanding over incomprehension,
forgiveness over offense,
love over hate.
Through Christ our Lord.
Amen.

Second Mystery

THE BIRTH OF JESUS IN BETHLEHEM
*With the birth of the Son of the Virgin
the gift of peace is offered to all men, near and far.*

WORD OF THE LORD
From the Gospel according to Luke (2:11, 13—14).

The angel said to the shepherds: "To you is born this day in the city of David a savior, who is Christ the Lord." And suddenly there was with the angel a multitude of the heavenly host praising God and saying, "Glory to God in the highest and on earth peace among men with whom he is pleased."

TEACHING OF THE CHURCH
From the Encyclical Pacem in Terris *of Pope John XXIII*
(April 11, 1963, No. 60).

"This is the peace that we ask of the Lord Jesus with the burning breath of our prayer. May he remove from the hearts of men that which endangers it; and may he transform them into witnesses of truth, justice, and brotherly love.

"May he enlighten the leaders of peoples, so that, in addition to their care for the proper well-being of their citizens, they may guarantee and defend the great gift of peace; may he inspire in all men the will to overcome the barriers that divide them, to increase the bonds of mutual charity, to understand others, to forgive those who have brought injustices; by virtue of his action, may all the peoples of the earth become brothers and may the much longed-for peace flourish among them and reign forever."

—Our Father
—Hail Mary
—Glory Be

PRAYER
God of our Fathers
Father of all,
who in your Son Jesus, the Prince of Peace,

give true peace to people near and far,
hear the petition that the Church addresses to you
together with the Mother of your Son:
help the soldiers on every front
who, forced by grievous decisions,
are fighting one another in the Gulf War;
free them from feelings of hatred and revenge,
enable them to keep in their hearts
the desire for peace,
so that when they are faced with the horrors of war
distress does not become for them
depression and desperation.
Through Christ our Lord.
Amen.

Third Mystery
THE DEATH OF JESUS ON THE CROSS
*With the death of Jesus every dividing wall was knocked down
and there was peace among peoples.*

WORD OF THE LORD
From the Gospel according to John (19:28–30).

Jesus, knowing that all was now finished, said (to fulfill the Scripture), "I thirst."... When Jesus had received the vinegar he said, "It is finished!" And he bowed his head and gave up his spirit.

TEACHING OF THE CHURCH
From the Pastoral Constitution Gaudium et Spes
of the Second Vatican Council (December 7, 1965, No. 78).

"That earthly peace which arises from love of neighbor sym-
bolizes and results from the peace of Christ which radiates
from God the Father. For by the Cross the Incarnate Son, the
Prince of Peace, reconciled all men with God. By thus restoring all men to the unity of one people and one body, he slew
hatred in his own flesh. . . .

"For this reason, all Christians are urgently summoned
to do in love what the truth requires, and to join with all
true peacemakers in pleading for peace and bringing it
about."

— Our Father
— Hail Mary
— Glory Be

PRAYER
Father,
your Son, the Holy, the innocent,
died on the Cross,
a victim of man's sin.
He died
soaking the earth with blood
and sowing in the hearts of men
words of forgiveness and peace.
Hear, O Father,

the cry of innocent blood
spilled on the battlefields,
and welcome into your dwelling of light,
through the maternal intercession of the Mother of
 sorrow,
those men whom the violence of weapons
has torn from life
and delivered into the hands of your mercy.
Through Christ our Lord.
Amen.

Fourth Mystery
THE RESURRECTION OF JESUS
*In the Resurrection of Christ
peace is communicated
to mankind and all creatures.*

WORD OF THE LORD
From the Gospel according to John (20:19–21).

On the evening of that day, the first day of the week…
Jesus came and stood among his Disciples and said to
them, "Peace be with you!" Then the Disciples were glad
when they saw the Lord. Jesus said to them again, "Peace
be with you!"

TEACHING OF THE CHURCH
*From the speech of Pope Paul VI to the General Assembly
of the United Nations (October 4, 1965, No. 5).*

"You are waiting for this word from us, which cannot but be clothed in gravity and solemnity: *never again one against another, never, never again!*

"It was principally for this purpose that the United Nations came into being; against war and for peace....

"It doesn't take many words to state the highest goal of this institution. We need only recall that the blood of millions of people and innumerable and unprecedented sufferings, useless slaughter and tremendous ruin ratify the pact that unites you, with an oath that must change the future history of the world: never again war, never again war!

"Peace, peace must guide the fate of peoples and of all humanity."

—Our Father
—Hail Mary
—Glory Be

PRAYER
Father, you who love life,
who in the Resurrection of your Son Jesus
have renewed man and all creation
and wish to bring them
peace as your first gift:
look with compassion
upon humanity torn apart by war;

save the creatures
of the sky, the earth, and the sea,
the work of your hands,
threatened by destruction among unprecedented
    sufferings,
and let peace alone, through the intercession of Holy
    Mary,
guide the fate
of peoples and of nations.
Through Jesus Christ our Lord.
Amen.

Fifth Mystery
THE DESCENT OF THE HOLY SPIRIT
*At Pentecost, the Spirit of God, the Spirit of peace and harmony,
was poured out over all peoples.*

WORD OF THE LORD
From the Acts of the Apostles (2:1, 4, 6, 9–11).

When the day of Pentecost had come ... the Disciples were all filled with the Holy Spirit and began to speak in other tongues. ... And the multitude were bewildered because each one heard them speaking in his own language....

Parthians and Medes and Elamites, and residents of Mesopotamia, Judea and Cappadocia, Pontus and Asia, Phrygia and Pamphylia, Egypt and the parts of Libya belonging to Cyrene, and visitors from Rome, both Jews and proselytes, Cretans and Arabians, we hear them telling in our own tongues the mighty works of God.

TEACHING OF THE CHURCH
From the Message Urbi et Orbi *of Pope John Paul II* (*Christmas, 1990*).

"The light of Christ shines on the tormented nations of the Middle East. Fearfully we wait for the threat of war to vanish from the region of the Gulf.

"Convince the leaders that war is an adventure that has no return! With reason, patience, and dialogue, and with respect for the inalienable rights of populations and peoples, it is possible that we may discover the pathways of understanding and peace, and follow them.

"The Holy Land, too, has been waiting many years for peace: a peaceful solution to the entire question that vexes it, a solution that takes account of the legitimate expectations of the Palestinian people and of those who live in the state of Israel."

— Our Father
— Hail Mary
— Glory Be

PRAYER
In this time of unprecedented violence
and useless slaughter,
hear, O Father,
the entreaty that goes up to you from all the Church,
as we pray with Mary, Queen of Peace:
instill in the governments of all nations
the Spirit of unity and harmony,
of love and peace,
so that the hoped-for message

may reach the ends of the earth:
War is over!
And, with the clash of arms silenced,
may hymns of peace and brotherhood echo throughout
    the earth.
Through Christ our Lord.
Amen.

— Salve Regina
— Litanies

Prayer for Peace

God of our Fathers,
mighty and merciful,
Lord of peace and life,
Father of all.

You have plans for peace, not violence,
you condemn war
and overthrow the pride of the aggressor.

You sent your Son Jesus
to declare peace near and far,
to unite men of every race and every creed
in a single family.
Hear the unanimous cry of your children,
the heartfelt petition of all humanity:
no more war, an adventure without return,
no more war, a spiral of grief and violence;
stop this war in the Persian Gulf,
this threat to your creatures
in the sky, on earth, and in the sea.

In communion with Mary, the Mother of Jesus,
again we entreat you:
speak to the hearts of those responsible for the fate of
    peoples,
stop the logic of reprisal and revenge,
through your Spirit suggest new solutions,

generous and honorable gestures,
space for dialogue and patient waiting:
more fruitful than the frenzied descent into war.

Grant in our time
days of peace.
No more war.
Amen.

FEBRUARY 2, 1991

A Rosary with young people

PRAYER

Let us pray.
O God, who through your only Son
have opened up to men the source of peace,
through the intercession of the Blessed Virgin Mary
give to men and women whom you love
the much desired, long-sought peace,
that they may form a single family
joined in the chain of fraternal charity.
Through Christ our Lord.
Amen.

First Mystery

THE ANNUNCIATION

*The meditation on the mystery of the Annunciation
is given by a group of young people.*

First reader: First mystery: let's contemplate the Angel Gabriel's message to Mary.

Second reader: From the Gospel according to Luke (1:26, 28–31, 38a).

The Angel Gabriel was sent by God to a virgin named Mary. "Hail," he said. "O favored one, the Lord is with you."

But she was greatly troubled at the saying.

And the angel said to her, "Do not be afraid, Mary. Behold, you will conceive in your womb and bear a son, and you shall call his name Jesus."

Then Mary said: "Behold, I am the handmaid of the Lord, let it be to me according to your word."

Third reader: In the womb of the Virgin Mary, your Son, O Father, became man, to reconcile men with you and with each other.

As it happened for Mary, O Lord, turn our lives to faithful and obedient service to you, for the life of the world.

— Our Father
— Hail Mary
— Glory Be

PRAYER

O God, who with the angel's message
willed that your Word
should be made man in the womb of the Virgin
    Mary,
may your people,
who worship her as the true Mother of God,
always have the joy of her intercession with you.
Through Christ our Lord.
Amen.

Second Mystery
THE RESURRECTION OF JESUS
*The meditation on the mystery of the Resurrection
is offered by some people who are ill.*

First reader: In the second mystery, we contemplate the Resurrection of Jesus.

Second reader: From the Gospel according to Matthew (28:1–2, 5–8).

Now after the Sabbath, toward the dawn of the first day of the week, Mary Magdalene and the other Mary went to see the sepulcher.

And behold, there was a great earthquake; for an angel of the Lord descended from Heaven, and came and rolled back the stone, and sat upon it.

But the angel said to the women, "Do not be afraid; for I know that you seek Jesus who was crucified. He is not here, for he has risen, as he said. Come, see the place where he lay. Then go quickly and tell his disciples that he is risen from the dead and behold, he is going before you to Galilee; there you will see him. Lo, I have told you."

So they departed quickly from the tomb with fear and great joy, and ran to tell his disciples.

Third reader: With the Resurrection of Christ, you, O Father, filled the heart of Mary with ineffable joy.

Allow us, too, strong in his joy, to contemplate forever the face of the Lord who is risen.

—Our Father
— Hail Mary
—Glory Be

PRAYER

O God, who in the glorious Resurrection of your Son
have given joy to all the world,
through the intercession of Mary the Virgin

grant us the joy of life without end.
Through Christ our Lord.
Amen.

Third Mystery

THE DESCENT OF THE HOLY SPIRIT
ON MARY AND THE APOSTLES
*The meditation on the mystery of Pentecost
is offered by a group of husbands and wives.*

First reader: In the third mystery, we contemplate the descent of the Holy Spirit upon Mary and the Apostles gathered in prayer in the Upper Room.

Second reader: From the Gospel according to John (20:19– 22).

On the evening of that day, the first day of the week, Jesus came and stood among them, and said to them, "Peace be with you!"

When he had said this, he showed them his hands and his side. Then the Disciples were glad when they saw the Lord.

Jesus said to them again, "Peace be with you! As the Father has sent me, even so I send you."

And when he had said this, he breathed on them and said to them, "Receive the Holy Spirit."

Third reader: You sent us your Son, Jesus, O Father, and through him you have given us the Holy Spirit. Shine his light and his peace into our hearts and enable us, following the example of Mary, to seek out, keep, and bear witness to the Word of life forever.

—Our Father
— Hail Mary
—Glory Be

PRAYER
O Father, who have poured the gifts of your Spirit
on the blessed Virgin
praying with the Apostles in the Upper Room,
let us persevere in prayer as one voice
with Mary our mother
to bring to the world, through the power of the Spirit,
the joyous news of salvation.
Through Christ our Lord.
Amen.

Act of Entrustment to the Virgin of Fatima, May 13, 1991

1. **Holy Mother of the Redeemer,**
Gate of Heaven, Star of the sea,
help your people, who yearn to rise.
Yet again
we turn to you,
Mother of Christ,
and of the Church.
We gather at your feet
to thank you
for what you have done
in these difficult years
for the Church,
for each of us,
and for all humanity.

2. **"Show thyself a Mother":**
How many times have we called on you!
And today we are here to thank you,
because you have always listened to us.
You showed that you are our mother:
Mother of the Church,
missionary along the paths of the earth
in expectation of the third Christian millennium.
Mother of men,
for the constant protection

that has averted disasters
and irreparable destruction,
and has encouraged progress
and improvements in modern society.
Mother of nations,
for the unhoped-for changes
that have given trust back to peoples
too long oppressed and humiliated.
Mother of life, for the many signs
with which you accompanied us,
defending us from evil
and from the power of death.
My mother forever,
and in particular on that May 13, 1981,
when I felt beside me
your succoring presence.
Mother of every man who struggles for the life
that does not die.
Mother of humanity
redeemed by the blood of Christ.
Mother of perfect love,
of hope and peace,
Holy Mother of the Redeemer.

3. "Show thyself a Mother":
Yes, continue to show that you are the mother of us all,
because the world needs you.
The new situations
of peoples and the Church
are still precarious and unstable.

The danger exists
of replacing Marxism
with another form of atheism,
which, idolizing freedom,
tends to destroy
the roots of human and Christian morality.
Mother of hope, walk with us!
Walk with mankind
at the very end
of the twentieth century,
with men of every race and culture,
of every age and state.
Walk with peoples
toward solidarity and love,
walk with the young,
the protagonists of future days of peace.
The nations that have recently
regained their freedom
and are now engaged
in constructing their future
have need of you.
Europe needs you,
which from east to west
cannot find
its identity
without rediscovering
its common Christian roots.
The world needs you
to resolve
the many violent

conflicts that still
threaten it.

4. "Show thyself a Mother":

Show that you are the mother of the poor,
of those who are dying of hunger and sickness,
of those who suffer injustice and tyranny,
of those who cannot find work, home, or refuge,
of those who are oppressed and exploited,
of those who despair or in vain seek
tranquillity far from God.
Help us to defend life,
the reflection of divine love,
help us to defend it forever,
from dawn to its natural sunset.
Show yourself the mother of unity and peace.
May violence and injustice cease everywhere,
may harmony and unity
grow within families,
and respect and understanding among peoples;
may peace, true peace, reign upon the earth!
Mary, give Christ, our peace, to the world.
Do not let peoples reopen new abysses
of hatred and vengeance,
do not let the world yield to the seductions
of a false well-being
that perverts the value of the human person
and forever compromises
the natural resources of creation.
Show yourself the mother of hope!

Watch over the road that still awaits us.
Watch over men
and over the new situations of peoples
still threatened by the risk of war.
Watch over those responsible for nations
and those who rule the destiny of humanity.
Watch over the Church,
which is constantly threatened by the spirit of the
    world.
Watch over, in particular,
the next special assembly
of the Synod of Bishops,
an important stop on the road
of the new evangelization in Europe.
Watch over my time in Peter's ministry,
in the service of the Gospel and of man
heading toward the new goals
of the missionary action of the Church.
Totus tuus!

5. In collegial unity with the Pastors, and
in communion with the entire people of God,
who are scattered to the far corners of the earth,
I today renew humanity's
filial trust in you.
To you we all confidently entrust ourselves.
With you we hope to follow Christ,
the Redeemer of man: may our weariness
not weigh on us, nor our toil slacken us;
let not obstacles quench our courage,

nor sadness the joy in our hearts.
You, Mary, Mother of the Redeemer,
continue to show that you are the Mother of all,
watch over our path,
so that, full of joy, we may see
your Son in Heaven.
Amen.

Holy Rosary

The theme of this Rosary is the celebration of some of the principal events in the story of salvation, taken from the New Testament, in which the Father, through his Son Jesus, in the Holy Spirit, with the collaboration of the Virgin Mary, wished to reveal to mankind his plan of salvation. Through Mary, and the Rosary, the Church contemplates the Mystery of Divine Mercy and, trusting in the maternal intercession of the Virgin, entreats the Father to continue to show his love and mercy toward those who appeal to him.

PRAYER
O God, Father of mercy,
who in Mary, the Mother of Christ your Son,
have given us a mother
always ready to come to our aid,
grant, we pray you,
that, by tirelessly asking for
her maternal protection,
we may be worthy to enjoy forever
the fruits of Redemption.
Through Christ our Lord.
Amen.

First Mystery

THE ANNUNCIATION

*In the virginal womb of Mary the living Word of the Father
became flesh to show God's mercy.*

WORD OF THE LORD

From the Gospel according to Luke (1:28, 31–33, 35c).

The angel came to her and said: "Hail, O favored one, the Lord
is with you.... Behold, you will conceive in your womb and
bear a son, and you shall call his name Jesus.... The Lord God
will give to him the throne of his father David and he will reign
over the house of Jacob forever; and of his kingdom there will
be no end. Therefore the child to be born will be called holy,
the Son of God."

TEACHING OF THE CHURCH

From the Encyclical Redemptor Hominis *of John Paul II (No. 1).*

We also are in a certain way in a season of a new Advent, a
season of expectation: "In many and various ways God spoke
of old to our fathers by the prophets; but in these last days he
has spoken to us by a Son," by the Son, his Word, who became
man and was born of the Virgin Mary. This act of Redemption marked the high point of the history of man within God's
loving plan. God entered the history of humanity. Through
the Incarnation God gave human life the dimension that he
intended man to have from his first beginning; he has granted
that dimension definitively, in the way that is peculiar to him
alone, in keeping with his eternal love and mercy.

—Our Father
—Hail Mary
—Glory Be

PRAYER

God of our fathers,
source of consolation and peace,
who with the Incarnation of your Son
in the pure womb of Mary
revealed your mercy
and brought reconciliation to the world,
allow every man
to work responsibly for peace
so that adventures without return may nevermore
threaten the creatures of the sky,
the earth, and the sea.
Through Christ our Lord.
Amen.

Second Mystery

MARY MEETS ELIZABETH
*In the meeting of Mary and Elizabeth the mercy
of the Lord is proclaimed for all the generations.*

WORD OF THE LORD

From the Gospel according to Luke (1:40–42, 46, 49 50).

Mary entered the house of Zechariah and greeted Elizabeth.
And when Elizabeth heard the greeting of Mary, the babe
leaped in her womb; and Elizabeth was filled with the Holy

Spirit and she exclaimed with a loud cry, "Blessed are you among women, and blessed is the fruit of your womb!" And Mary said, "My soul magnifies the Lord. He who is mighty has done great things for me and holy is his name. And his mercy is on those who fear him from generation to generation."

TEACHING OF THE CHURCH
From the Encyclical Dives in Misericordia
of John Paul II (No. 10, 12).

We have every right to believe that our generation, too, was included in the words of the Mother of God when she glorified that mercy shared in "from generation to generation" by those who allow themselves to be guided by the fear of God. The words of Mary's Magnificat have a prophetic content that concerns not only the past of Israel but also the whole future of the People of God on earth. In fact, all of us now living on earth are the generation that is aware of the approach of the third millennium and profoundly feels the change that is occurring in history.

The Church of our time, constantly pondering the eloquence of these words inspired by Mary, and applying them to the sufferings of the great human family, must become more particularly and profoundly conscious of the need to bear witness to God's mercy in its whole mission.

— Our Father
— Hail Mary
— Glory Be

PRAYER

We magnify you, Almighty Lord,
with hymns of exultation and praise: in the Virgin
    Mary
you demonstrate to all the generations how the one
    who is
evangelized becomes the evangelizer,
how the joyful news of freedom
becomes works
of caring and generous charity;
now we pray to you that
the Churches of East and West
may devote themselves decisively
with words and deeds
to the poor and the humble.
Through Christ our Lord.
Amen.

Third Mystery

THE MARRIAGE AT CANA

*At the marriage of Cana the intervention of Mary
obtains the gift of love for the newlywed couple.*

WORD OF THE LORD

From the Gospel according to John (2:1–5).

On the third day, there was a marriage at Cana in Galilee, and
the mother of Jesus was there. Jesus, also, was invited to the
marriage with his Disciples. When the wine failed, the mother
of Jesus said to him: "They have no wine." And Jesus said to

her, "O woman, what have you to do with me? My hour has not yet come." His mother said to the servants: "Do whatever he tells you."

TEACHING OF THE CHURCH
From the Encyclical Redemptoris Mater *of John Paul II (No. 21).*

At Cana in Galilee only one concrete aspect of human need is demonstrated, and it is apparently small and of little importance ("They have no wine"). But it has a symbolic value: this coming to the aid of human needs means, at the same time, bringing those needs within the radius of Christ's messianic mission and power of salvation. Thus there is a mediation: Mary places herself between her Son and mankind in the reality of man's wants, needs, and sufferings. And that is not all. As a mother she also wishes the messianic power of her Son to be manifested, that power of salvation of his which is meant to help man in his misfortunes, to free him from the evil that in various forms and degrees weighs heavily upon his life.

— Our Father
— Hail Mary
— Glory Be

PRAYER
Holy Father,
at Cana in Galilee
you wanted your Son
through the merciful intercession of Mary

to meet the needs of man
by performing for the young husband and wife
the first of his many miracles;
hear the prayer that the Church addresses to you
in communion with the Mother of your Son:
continue to pour forth
upon our young people,
upon Christian families, upon troubled couples
the gifts of your holy Spirit
so that their generosity and their love
may grow and expand from day to day.
Through Christ our Lord.
Amen.

Fourth Mystery
THE GLORIOUS DEATH OF JESUS ON THE CROSS
The glorious death of Jesus reveals the fullness of divine mercy.

WORD OF THE LORD
From the Gospel according to John (19:25–27, 30b).

Standing by the Cross of Jesus were his mother, and his mother's sister, Mary the wife of Clopas, and Mary Magdalene. When Jesus saw his mother, and the Disciple whom he loved standing near, he said to his mother, "Woman, behold your son!" Then he said to the Disciple, "Behold your mother!" And from that hour the Disciple took her to his own home. After this, Jesus, knowing that all was now finished, said, "It is finished!"; and he bowed his head and gave up his spirit.

TEACHING OF THE CHURCH
From the Encyclical Dives in Misericordia *of John Paul II (No. 9).*

Mary is the one who obtained mercy in a particular and exceptional way, as no other person has. At the same time, still in an exceptional way, she made possible with the sacrifice of her heart her own sharing in revealing God's mercy. This sacrifice is intimately linked with the Cross of her Son, at the foot of which she was to stand on Calvary. No one has experienced, to the same degree as the Mother of the crucified One, the Mystery of the Cross, the overwhelming encounter of divine transcendent justice with love: that "kiss" given by mercy to justice. No one has received into his heart, as much as Mary did, that Mystery, that truly divine dimension of the Redemption effected on Calvary by means of the death of the Son, together with the sacrifice of her mother's heart, together with her definitive "yes."

— Our Father
— Hail Mary
— Glory Be

PRAYER
Merciful and compassionate God,
in your great love
you wanted the Mother to be present
at the Cross of your Son;
look kindly on our brothers and sisters who are
    suffering:
in the light of the Resurrection of the Only Begotten

may the hope that life
is stronger than death never fail,
and grant that we may,
like Mary, our mother,
stand by the infinite crosses of men
to bring them comfort and consolation.
Through Christ our Lord.
Amen.

Fifth Mystery

THE DESCENT OF THE HOLY SPIRIT
At Pentecost, the spirit of God, the spirit of comfort
and mercy, poured down on Mary praying with the Disciples.

WORD OF THE LORD
From the Acts of the Apostles (1:12, 13a, 14; 2:1–4a).

The Apostles returned to Jerusalem from the mount called
Olivet. And when they had entered, they went up to the Upper
Room, where they were staying. All these with one accord
devoted themselves to prayer, together with the women and
Mary, the Mother of Jesus, and with his brothers. When the
day of Pentecost had come, suddenly a sound came from
Heaven like the rush of a mighty wind, and it filled all the
house where they were sitting. And there appeared to them
tongues as of fire, distributing and resting on each one of
them. And they were all filled with the Holy Spirit.

TEACHING OF THE CHURCH
From the Encyclical Redemptoris Mater *of John Paul II (No. 40).*

After the events of the Resurrection and Ascension, Mary entered the Upper Room together with the Apostles to await Pentecost, and was present there as the Mother of the glorified Lord. She was not only the one who "advanced in her pilgrimage of faith" and loyally persevered in her union with her Son "unto the Cross," but she was also the "handmaid of the Lord," left by her Son as Mother in the midst of the infant Church: "Behold your mother." After her Son's departure, her motherhood remains in the Church as mediator: interceding for all her children, the Mother cooperates in the saving work of her Son, the Redeemer of the world.

— Our Father
— Hail Mary
— Glory Be

PRAYER
Almighty God,
lover of life,
we, like the Apostles on the day of Pentecost,
are in prayerful communion
with Mary, the Mother of your Son;
as supplicants we ask you
to renew in all and in each
the gifts of the Consoler,
so that, comforted by his presence,
we may proclaim your mercy

and communicate it with our lives
to all creatures.
Through Christ our Lord.
Amen.

Meditation

In reciting the Rosary, we have repeated with faith the words
of the angel, *"Hail Mary,"* and of St. Elizabeth, *"Blessed are you
among women,"* reliving the same attitude of loving trust that your
forebears had toward her, the Mother of the Redeemer. In difficult and sometimes tragic situations, in times of catastrophe,
invasion, and war, they were able to find, in their faith in God
the Father, in Jesus Christ the Redeemer, and in the Holy Spirit,
love, the foundation of fearless strength, which sustained them,
nourishing their hope in unfailing divine intervention.

In every *Hail Mary* they recalled the mysterious gift made by
God to man, to every man, in the Incarnation of the Word, and
they knew very well that the condition of this mortal life can
find support and protection in the Mother of God, since it is
Mary who gave the Savior to the world, and who with bound-
less affection prays for us sinners *"now and in the hour of our death."*

Like them, we, too, in the *Hail Mary*, this simple prayer that
children learn on their mother's knee, call on the Virgin full of
grace, we entrust ourselves to her intercession, we bless her
divine Son, the fruit of her womb, echoing the words of the
Gospel: *"Blessed is the womb that bore you, the breast that suckled you."*
We declare, similarly, that her maternal aid is indispensable to
us at the fundamental moments of our existence: in the present
and in the "hour of our death," the decisive moment of passage
to eternal life.

These simple considerations offer us the opportunity to reflect briefly on the importance of prayer: public and liturgical, private, personal, and familial; the prayer that we say aloud, repeating ancient and venerable words, and the one that goes silently up from the heart, accompanied by the most profound emotions of our soul.

The Rosary, in a special way, with its meditations on the mysteries, engages one's full expressive capacity in oral prayer. As we relive the moments of joy and sorrow in the life of Christ and his Immaculate Mother, our spirit is nourished, which leads us to dialogue with the Lord and to contemplation. In the Rosary we also recall our human condition marked by sin and ask for divine forgiveness. We ask for the graces that we need: first of all that we may escape evil and live in friendship with the Lord, in accordance with his Gospel. The life of the Redeemer, miraculously marked by the power of the Father and the living presence of the Holy Spirit, appears to us, through the Joyful, Sorrowful, and Glorious Mysteries, as the model of our baptismal vocation, directed to the imitation and following of the divine Teacher.

The Marian prayer, then, is an interior pilgrimage that leads the believer, with the help of the Virgin, to the spiritual mountain of holiness. It is the school of ecclesial communion, in the hearing of the one who occupies in the Church the place that is highest and closest to Christ. Mary is the model of hardworking charity, since, "embracing with all her soul and with no burden of sin the saving will of God, she devoted herself completely as the handmaid of the Lord to the person and the work of her Son, helping in the mystery of Redemption dependent on him and with him, by the grace of Almighty

God." Mary is the image and the origin of the Church, and she remains vitally joined to it through her communion with the Redeemer. We cannot, therefore, think of living in true devotion to Our Lady if we are not in full harmony with the Church and its Bishop. If we do not take care to be, at the same time, an obedient child of the Church, whose duty it is to verify the legitimacy of the various forms of religious feeling, we would be deluding ourselves that she hears us as her child. It is not by chance that the Second Vatican Council warned, with all the solemnity of its teaching authority, "The faithful must remember that true devotion does not consist in a sterile and transient feeling, or in a secure yet vain credulity, but, rather, proceeds from true faith."

Dear brothers and sisters, as your fathers, more than five hundred years ago, climbed this Hill as penitents, aware of their own misery but exultant because they had been assured by their Bishop of the merciful intercession of Mary, so, too, we have now come to the foot of it, inspired by our great trust. "Mary is present in the Church as the Mother of Christ . . . and embraces with her new maternity in the Spirit all and each of us in the Church, embraces all and each of us through the Church."

"Show thyself a Mother," your fathers wrote under the image of Our Lady of Mount Berico.* "Show thyself a Mother," we, too, repeat, affectionately, conscious of the deep bond that exists between the Mother of Christ and the Church, between love for Christ and love for the Church. As we know, Mary,

---

*The shrine of Our Lady of Mount Berico is on a hill outside Vicenza. It is a place of Marian devotion and pilgrimage, kept by the Friar Servants of Mary.

who was "present in the mystery of Christ, is constantly present in the mystery of the Church as well." Comforted by that truth, we wish to be, in turn, her devoted children, by remaining faithful children of the Church, in line with the Christian generations that have preceded us. We wish to love Mary in the present and in eternal life.

O Mary,
turn your merciful gaze toward us.
Show thyself a mother!
Show thyself the mother of those who suffer
and long for justice and peace.
"Show thyself the mother of every man
who struggles for the life that does not die.
Mother of humanity
redeemed by the blood of Christ:
Mother of perfect love,
of hope and peace,
Holy Mother of the Redeemer."
Show thyself our mother,
the mother of unity and hope,
while with the whole Church we cry out to you again:
"Mother of mercy,
our life, our sweetness, and our hope . . .
after this our exile show unto us
the blessed fruit of your womb, Jesus!
O clement, O loving,
O sweet Virgin Mary."

Holy Rosary

PRAYER

O God, who in the glorious Resurrection of your Son
gave joy back to the entire world,
through the intercession of the Virgin Mary,
grant that we who, tirelessly asking for
her maternal intercession,
may have the joy of life without end.
Through our Lord Jesus Christ,
your Son, who is God,
and lives and reigns with you, in the unity of the Holy
   Spirit,
forever and ever.
Amen.

First Mystery

THE ANNUNCIATION
*In the virginal womb of Mary the living
Word of the Father was incarnated to reveal God's mercy.*

WORD OF THE LORD
From the Gospel according to Luke (Luke 1:28, 31).

The angel came to her and said: "Hail, O favored one, the
Lord is with you. . . . Behold, you will conceive in your womb
and bear a son, and you shall call his name Jesus."

—Our Father
—Hail Mary
—Glory Be

PRAYER

O God of our fathers,
who with the angel's message
willed that your word
should become man in the virgin womb of Mary,
let your people, who worship her
as the true Mother of God,
find consistently in docile
acceptance of your Word
the strength to bear witness of it to all peoples.
Through Christ our Lord.
Amen.

Second Mystery

THE MEETING

*In the meeting of Mary and Elizabeth the Lord's
mercy is proclaimed for all the generations.*

WORD OF THE LORD

From the Gospel according to Luke (Luke 1:40–42, 46, 49–50).

Mary entered the house of Zechariah and greeted Elizabeth. And when Elizabeth heard the greeting of Mary, the babe leaped in her womb; and Elizabeth was filled with the Holy Spirit and she exclaimed with a loud cry, "Blessed are you among women, and blessed is the fruit of your womb!"

And Mary said, "My soul magnifies the Lord. He who is mighty has done great things for me and holy is his name. And his mercy is on those who fear him from generation to generation."

— Our Father
— Hail Mary
— Glory Be

PRAYER

O God, Savior of all peoples,
who through the blessed Virgin Mary,
ark of the new covenant,
brought salvation and joy
to the house of Elizabeth,
let our Church, obedient to the action
of the Spirit, undertake to bear witness to
the Gospel with words and charity.
Through Christ our Lord.
Amen.

Third Mystery

*The motherly presence of Mary at the first
miracle of Christ at Cana in Galilee.*

WORD OF THE LORD
From the Gospel according to John (John 2:1–5).

On the third day, there was a marriage at Cana in Galilee, and the mother of Jesus was there. Jesus, also, was invited to the marriage with his Disciples. When the wine failed, the mother of Jesus said to him: "They have no wine." And Jesus said to her, "O woman, what have you to do with me? My hour has not yet come." His mother said to the servants: "Do whatever he tells you."

—Our Father
—Hail Mary
—Glory Be

PRAYER

O Father, who in your miraculous providence
wished to join the Virgin Mary
to the mystery of our salvation,
let us, accepting the Mother's invitation,
trustfully approach
the Eucharistic Feast
which is the source of true joy.
In particular help newlywed husbands and wives,
Christian families,

142

couples in trouble,
so that their love may grow from day to day.
Through Christ our Lord.
Amen.

Fourth Mystery
THE RESURRECTION
The Resurrection of Jesus offers all men and women the gift of true life.

WORD OF THE LORD
From the Gospel according to Matthew (Matthew 28:5–7).

But the angel said to the women, "Do not be afraid; for I
know that you seek Jesus who was crucified. He is not here,
for he has risen, as he said. Come, see the place where he lay.
Then go quickly and tell his disciples that he is risen from
the dead."

—Our Father
—Hail Mary
—Glory Be

PRAYER
O God, Lord of life and history,
who raised your Only Begotten Son
to the glory of Heaven,
and wanted his Mother
to share in this fullness,
confirm our faith in the blessed Resurrection
so that with this hope we may

143

advance on the road of salvation.
Through Christ our Lord.
Amen.

Fifth Mystery
THE EFFUSION OF THE SPIRIT
At Pentecost the Spirit of God, the spirit of consolation and mercy,
pours down upon Mary praying with the disciples.

WORD OF THE LORD
From the Gospel according to John (John 15:26–27).

When the Counselor comes, whom I shall send to you from
the Father, even the Spirit of Truth, who proceeds from the
Father, he will bear witness to me, and you also are witnesses,
because you have been with me from the beginning.

—Our Father
—Hail Mary
—Glory Be

PRAYER
O Father, who poured down the gifts of your Spirit
on the blessed Virgin
as she prayed with the Apostles in the Upper Room,
let us persevere as one voice in prayer
with Mary our mother
to bring to the world, with the force of the Spirit,
the gift of your consolation,
the happy news of salvation.
Through Christ our Lord.
Amen.

Act of Entrustment to Our Lady

Assembly:
O Mary, Mother of Jesus and our mother,
we are gathered here as a community
united in love before you,
the living presence of the Church
and the sure sign of hope
for the pilgrim people of God.

Leader:
Recognizing your mission
in the story of salvation
and accepting you as a precious gift
of Christ who was crucified,
we hail you with the Angel Gabriel.

Assembly:
Rejoice, O favored one,
the Lord is with you!

Leader:
With Elizabeth we acclaim you.

Assembly:
Blessed are you among women
And blessed is the fruit of your womb, Jesus.

Leader:
We praise you with all the people.

Assembly:
Blessed are you, Mary:
God has done great things in you.

Leader:
With the Christians of all eras
we address to you the ancient prayer.

Assembly:
Under your protection we seek refuge,
Holy Mother of God.
Do not scorn the entreaties
of us in our time of trial,
but free us from every danger,
O glorious blessed Virgin.
(brief silence)

Act of Entrustment

Assembly:
The distressing situation of the world and the divine mercy
that Christian people experience, O Mary, impel us to entrust
ourselves to you and to ask for your intercession with Jesus,
your Son and our Savior.

We renew the Act of Entrustment and consecrate ourselves,
our communities, and our peoples to your Immaculate Heart.

Leader:
Knowing that Jesus
entrusted us to your maternal care
in the person of the favored Disciple,

Assembly:
We entrust ourselves to you, Mary!

Leader:
So that you may help us to faithfully live
the tasks imposed by baptism,

Assembly:
We entrust ourselves to you, Mary!

Leader:
So that you may teach us to confide in the Lord
and in the saving power of Redemption,

Assembly:
We entrust ourselves to you, Mary!

Leader:
So that our Redemption
may always follow the paths of progress,
justice, and peace:

Assembly:
We entrust ourselves to you, Mary!

Leader:
So that our ecclesial community
may grow in fellowship
and be faithful to its mission of salvation:

Assembly:
We entrust ourselves to you, Mary!
(brief silence)

PETITION

Assembly:
Knowing that this Act of Entrustment requires a life in harmony with the Gospel, of which your life, O Mary, is a faithful reflection, we promise to live in imitation of your faith in order to radiate peace, brotherhood, and love.

But since without the help of the Lord we would build in vain, we need to appeal to him, along with you, his Immaculate Mother.

Thinking of the experiences of the past, the needs of the present, and the threats of the future, we entreat you, Mary, to obtain for us from the Lord deliverance from every evil.

PRAYER

O God, who in your only Son
opened up to men the source of peace,
through the intercession of the Blessed Virgin Mary,
give to men and women whom you love
the much-desired, long-sought peace,

so that we may all be a single family
united in the chain of fraternal charity.
Through Christ our Lord.
Amen.

Rosary for vocations

The Joyful Mysteries
THE VOCATION OF MARY

1. The Annunciation (Luke 1:26–38)
Mary's "yes" was above all an act of generosity, not only toward God but also toward men and women.

Let us pray: that children and young people may be attentive and generous to God's calls.

2. The Visitation (Luke 1:39–45)
Mary's gesture of putting herself "at the service of" Elizabeth was the result of her "yes" to God.

Let us pray: that the testimony of the permanent deacons and the consecrated in the secular institutes may be fruitful.

3. The Nativity (Luke 2:1–7)
God became man so that man might become like God. He is our brother in joy and sorrow.

Let us pray: for all those who offer their lives to share the lives of the poorest.

4. The Presentation in the Temple (Luke 2:22–35)
Parents who offer a child to God do not lose him, except to find him again transformed and enriched by grace.

Let us pray: that Christian families may be generous and open to every vocation.

5. The Finding (Luke 2:41–52)

The plans of the Lord are at times difficult to understand; they require acceptance, faith, and humility.

Let us pray: for the seminarians who are preparing for consecration.

The Sorrowful Mysteries
THE VOCATION OF JESUS

1. The Agony in the Garden (Luke 22:40–44)

Even at the time of our hardest trials, the Father waits and supports our "yes" to his will.

Let us pray: that the Father may give the gift of perseverance to those who have consecrated themselves to him entirely.

2. The Scourging (Mark 15:11–15)

Faithfulness to our vocation is needed to overcome others' lack of understanding and their attempts to discourage us.

Let us pray: for those who suffer persecution because of the Gospel.

3. The Crown of Thorns (Mark 15:17–20)

Sometimes suffering becomes part of our life as a true vocation.

Let us pray: that the sick will unite their suffering to the redeeming Passion of Christ.

4. The Condemnation to Death (John 19:13–16)

Often, the circumstances of life are a call from God to share the journey of our brothers.

Let us pray: that every Christian may feel responsible for the salvation of the world.

5. Crucifixion and Death (John 19:28–30)

If someone wants to follow Christ, he must renounce himself and take up the cross.

Let us pray: that men and women religious and those who live a contemplative life will adhere fully to their consecration.

The Glorious Mysteries
THE VOCATION OF THE CHURCH

1. The Resurrection (Mark 16: 9–14)

Today, as he was yesterday and always will be, he is the Risen One, the God of life and joy, to whom we are all called.

Let us pray: that Christian spouses may live God's love and be open to the gift of life.

2. The Ascension (Mark 16:15–19)

God needs our help to construct a world according to the Gospel.

Let us pray: that the priests in the Church may be numerous and holy.

3. The Pentecost (Acts 1:14, 2:2–4)

The Holy Spirit in us is the strength and courage to defend and spread the message of the Gospel.

Let us pray: that, through the testimony of missionaries, the missionary zeal of the Church may be constantly renewed.

4. The Assumption of Mary (Apocalypse 12:1)

Our earthly life, lived in faith, is destined for the glory of Heaven.

Let us pray: that those who are disappointed by life may find Christian hope.

5. The Crowning of Mary (Luke 1:30–33)

Even today Mary intercedes for our bewildered world and for the urgent needs of the Church.

Let us pray: that the Kingdom of God may be fulfilled.

A prayer to Mary from seminarians and priests

O Mother,
Mother of God,
Mother of the Church,
in this hour so significant for us
we are one heart and one soul:
like Peter, the Apostles, our brothers and sisters,
joined in prayer, with you,
in the Upper Room.

We entrust our life to you,
to you who welcomed in total faithfulness
the Word of God
and devoted yourself to his plan
of salvation and grace,
adhering with complete obedience
to the action of the Holy Spirit;
to you, who received from your Son
the mission to welcome and watch over
the Disciple he loved;
to you we repeat, each of us,
I am wholly yours,
so that you may take on our consecration
and join it to that of Jesus and to yours,
as an offering to God the Father,
for the life of the world.

We implore you, watch over
the needs of your children,
as you did at Cana, when you took to heart
the situation of that family.
What your family needs most today
is vocations: presbyterial,
deaconal, religious, and missionary.

With your "suppliant omnipotence,"
touch the hearts of our brothers,
so that they may hear, understand,
respond to the voice of the Lord.

Repeat to them,
in the depths of their conscience,
the command given to the servants at Cana:
"Do whatever Jesus tells you."

We will be ministers of God and of the Church,
vowed to evangelize, sanctify,
nourish our brothers and sisters:
teach us, give us
the habits of the Good Shepherd;
nurture our apostolic devotion and make it grow;
fortify and constantly regenerate
our love for those who suffer;
enlighten and vivify our offering
of virginity for the Kingdom of Heaven;
instill and preserve in us
the sense of fraternity and communion.

Along with our own lives we entrust to you,
O our Mother,
those of our parents and families;
those of our brothers and sisters whom we will reach
with our ministry,
so that your motherly concern
may precede our steps toward them
and keep our path directed toward the promised land,
which Christ, your Son and our Lord,
has prepared for us with his Redemption.
Amen.

APRIL 18, 1982

A prayer to Mary for priests

O Mary,
Mother of Jesus Christ and Mother of priests,
accept this title that we bestow on you
to celebrate your motherhood
and to contemplate with you the priesthood
of your Son and of your sons,
O Holy Mother of God.

O Mother of Christ,
to the Messiah-priest you gave a body of flesh
through the anointing of the Holy Spirit
for the salvation of the poor and the contrite of heart;
guard priests in your heart and in the Church,
O Mother of the Savior.

O Mother of Faith,
you accompanied to the temple the Son of Man,
the fulfillment of the promises given to the fathers;
give to the Father for his glory
the priests of your Son,
O Ark of the Covenant.

O Mother of the Church,
in the midst of the Disciples in the Upper Room
you prayed to the Spirit
for the new people and their shepherds;

obtain for the Order of Presbyters
a full measure of gifts,
O Queen of the Apostles.

O Mother of Jesus Christ,
you were with him at the beginning
of his life and mission,
you sought the Master among the crowd,
you stood beside him when he was lifted
up from the earth
consumed as the one eternal sacrifice,
and you had John, your son, near at hand;
accept from the beginning those
who have been called,
protect their growth,
in their life ministry accompany
your sons,
O Mother of Priests.
Amen.

PASTORES DABO VOBIS
(APOSTOLIC EXHORTATION, MARCH 25, 1992)

A prayer to Mary for vocations

O Virgin Mary,
to you we entrust our young people,
in particular those who are
called to follow your Son more closely.

You know the difficulties,
the struggles, the obstacles
they must face.

Assist them
to utter
their "yes" to the divine call,
as you did at the invitation of the angel.

Draw them to your heart
so that they can understand with you
the beauty and the joy that await them
when the Omnipotent calls them into his intimacy,
to make them witnesses of his Love
and make them able to inspire the Church
with their consecration.

O Virgin Mary, help us to rejoice with you
in seeing the love brought by your Son
received, treasured, and returned.

Grant that we
may see even in our own days
the wonders of the mysterious action
of the Holy Spirit.

MESSAGE FOR THE WORLD DAY OF
PRAYER FOR VOCATIONS, 1992

Prayer for lay people

O Most Blessed Virgin Mary,
Mother of Christ and Mother of the Church,
With joy and wonder we seek to make our own
your Magnificat, joining you in
your hymn of thankfulness and love.

With you we give thanks to God,
"whose mercy
is from generation to generation,"
for the exalted vocation
and the many forms of mission
entrusted to the lay faithful.
God has called each of them by name
to live his own communion of love
and holiness
and to be one
in the great family of God's children.
He has sent them forth
to shine with the light of Christ
and to communicate the fire of the Spirit
in every part of society
through their life
inspired by the Gospel.

O Virgin of the Magnificat,
fill their hearts

with gratitude and enthusiasm
for this vocation and mission.

With humility and magnanimity
you were the "handmaid of the Lord";
give us your unreserved willingness
for service to God
and the salvation of the world.
Open our eyes
to the great anticipation
of the Kingdom of God
and of the proclamation of the Gospel
to the whole of creation.

Your mother's heart
is ever mindful of the many dangers
and evils which threaten
to overpower men and women
in our time.
At the same time your heart also takes notice
of the many initiatives
undertaken for good,
the great yearning for values,
and the progress achieved
in bringing forth
the abundant fruits of salvation.

O Virgin full of courage,
may your spiritual strength
and trust in God inspire us,

so that we might know
how to overcome all the obstacles
that we encounter
in accomplishing our mission.
Teach us to treat the affairs
of the world
with a real sense of Christian responsibility
and a joyful hope
of the coming of God's Kingdom, and
of a "new Heaven and a new earth."

You who were together in prayer
with the Apostles in the Upper Room,
awaiting the coming
of the Spirit at Pentecost,
implore his renewed outpouring
on all the faithful, men and women alike,
so that they may more fully respond
to their vocation and mission,
as branches engrafted to the true vine,
called to bear much fruit
for the life of the world.

O Virgin Mother,
guide and sustain us
so that we may always live
as true sons and daughters
of the Church of your Son.
Enable us to do our part
in helping to establish on earth

the civilization of truth and love,
as God wills it,
for his glory.
Amen.

CHRISTIFIDELIS LAICI
(APOSTOLIC EXHORTATION,
DECEMBER 30, 1988)

To Mary, star of evangelization

O Mary, on the morning of Pentecost
you supported with prayer
the start of the evangelization
undertaken by the Apostles
through the action of the Holy Spirit.
With your constant protection
continue to guide today,
in these times of apprehension and hope,
the steps of the Church, which,
obedient to the mandate of the Lord,
goes out with the "good news" of salvation
to people and nations
in every corner of the earth.
Direct our choices in life,
comfort us in our time of trial,
so that, faithful to God and man,
we may face with humble courage
the mysterious paths of the ether,
and carry to the heart and mind of every person
the joyous news of Christ
the Redeemer of man.
O Mary, star of evangelization,
walk with us!
Amen.

OCTOBER 21, 1992

Mary, mediator of vocations

To you we turn, Mother of the Church.

To you who, with your "let it be," opened the door to the presence of Christ in the world, in history, and in individuals, accepting in humble silence and total availability the call of the Almighty.

Enable many men and women to hear again the inviting voice of your Son: "Follow me!"

Enable them to find the courage to leave their families, their occupations, their earthly hopes and follow Christ on his path.

Extend your maternal hand to the missionaries scattered all over the world, to the men and women religious who help the old, the sick, the lame, the orphans; to those who are engaged in teaching, to the members of secular institutes, silent fermenters of good works; to those who in closed communities live on faith and love and pray for the salvation of the world. Amen.

MESSAGE FOR THE WORLD DAY OF
PRAYER FOR VOCATIONS, 1988

Litany prayer

Lord, have mercy	Lord, have mercy
Christ, have mercy	Christ, have mercy
Lord, have mercy	Lord, have mercy
Holy Mary	pray for us
Holy Mother of God	pray for us
Holy Virgin of virgins	pray for us
Daughter beloved of the Father	pray for us
Mother of Christ, King of the Ages	pray for us
Glory of the Holy Spirit	pray for us
Virgin daughter of Zion	pray for us
Virgin poor and humble	pray for us
Virgin meek and mild	pray for us
Servant obedient in faith	pray for us
Mother of the Lord	pray for us
Cooperator of the Redeemer	pray for us
Full of grace	pray for us
Source of beauty	pray for us
Treasure of virtue and wisdom	pray for us
First fruit of the Redemption	pray for us
Perfect disciple of Christ	pray for us
Purest image of the Church	pray for us

Woman of the new covenant	pray for us
Woman clothed in sun	pray for us
Woman crowned with stars	pray for us
Lady of immense bounty	pray for us
Lady of forgiveness	pray for us
Lady of our families	pray for us
Joy of the new Israel	pray for us
Splendor of the Holy Church	pray for us
Honor of the human race	pray for us
Advocate of grace	pray for us
Minister of divine mercy	pray for us
Help of God's people	pray for us
Queen of love	pray for us
Queen of mercy	pray for us
Queen of peace	pray for us
Queen of the angels	pray for us
Queen of the patriarchs	pray for us
Queen of the prophets	pray for us
Queen of the Apostles	pray for us
Queen of the martyrs	pray for us
Queen of the confessors of the faith	pray for us
Queen of virgins	pray for us
Queen of all the saints	pray for us
Queen conceived without sin	pray for us
Queen assumed into Heaven	pray for us

Queen of the earth	pray for us
Queen of Heaven	pray for us
Queen of the universe	pray for us

Lamb of God
who take away the sins of the world,   forgive us, Lord.
Lamb of God
who take away the sins of the world,   hear us, Lord.
Lamb of God
who take away the sins of the world,   have pity on us.

Pray for us, glorious Mother of the Lord.
Make us worthy of Christ's promises.

Merciful God,
hear the prayer of your people
who honor with solemn rites
the Blessed Virgin Mary, your servant,
as mother and queen,
and grant that we may serve you and our brothers
in this world
to enter into the eternal dwelling of your kingdom.
Through Christ our Lord.
Amen.

Litanies of Loreto

Holy Mother of God	pray for us
Holy Virgin of virgins	pray for us
Mother of Christ	pray for us
Mother of the Church	pray for us
Mother of divine grace	pray for us
Mother most pure	pray for us
Mother most chaste	pray for us
Mother undefiled	pray for us
Mother immaculate	pray for us
Mother worthy of love	pray for us
Mother most admirable	pray for us
Mother of good counsel	pray for us
Mother of the Creator	pray for us
Mother of the Savior	pray for us
Prudent Virgin	pray for us
Virgin deserving of honor	pray for us
Virgin deserving of praise	pray for us
Powerful Virgin	pray for us
Clement Virgin	pray for us
Faithful Virgin	pray for us
Mirror of perfection	pray for us
Seat of Wisdom	pray for us
Source of our joy	pray for us
Temple of the Holy Spirit	pray for us

Tabernacle of eternal glory	pray for us
Dwelling consecrated to God	pray for us
Mystical rose	pray for us
Tower of the holy city of David	pray for us
Impregnable fortress	pray for us
Sanctuary of the Divine presence	pray for us
Ark of the covenant	pray for us
Gate of Heaven	pray for us
Morning star	pray for us
Health of the sick	pray for us
Refuge of sinners	pray for us
Comforter of the afflicted	pray for us
Help of Christians	pray for us
Queen of the angels	pray for us
Queen of the patriarchs	pray for us
Queen of the prophets	pray for us
Queen of the Apostles	pray for us
Queen of the martyrs	pray for us
Queen of the confessors of the faith	pray for us
Queen of virgins	pray for us
Queen of all the saints	pray for us
Queen conceived without sin	pray for us
Queen assumed into Heaven	pray for us
Queen of the earth	pray for us
Queen of the Rosary	pray for us
Queen of peace	pray for us

Conclusion

I would like to make many recommendations,
but I will leave you with one that is essential:
continue to love the Holy Rosary
and spread its practice
wherever you happen to be.

It is a prayer
that forms you in the school of the living Gospel
educates your soul to piety,
makes you persevere in the good,
prepares you for life, and,
above all,
makes you dear to Most Holy Mary,
who will protect you
and defend you from evil.

Pray to Our Lady for me, too,
while I entrust each of you
to her maternal protection.

MARCH 3, 1984

Special thanks to Stanley Browne, Martin Schmukler, Esq., and Marvin Kaplan of Marstan Associates, Ltd. Thanks also to the Libreria Editrice Rogate (LER), Father Nunzio Spinelli, and the Very Reverend Father Leonardo Sapienza, respectively, for the publication and the compilation of the anthologies. And to Rick Garson, Enzo Zullo, Alan R. Kershaw, Advocate of the Apostolic Tribunal of the Roman Rota, Paul Schindler, Esq., Larry Shire, Esq,. Gil Karson, Esq., of Grubman, Indusrky and Schindler.

KAROL WOJTYLA, POPE JOHN PAUL II, was born in Wadowice in Poland, in 1920. He studied literature and drama in Krakow and later worked at a stone quarry and at a chemical plant. During the German occupation of Poland in World War II, he began preparing for the priesthood and was ordained in 1946 Wojtyla became bishop of Krakow in 1958, archbishop in 1964, and cardinal in 1967. He was elected Pope in 1978 and is the 264th bishop of Rome.